Maximize Your Brain

A Hypnosis Handbook

John Cressman, C.Ht., C.S.H.

Maximize Your Brain

ISBN 978-0-9844087-2-6

This book is dedicated to my father, John, who has sacrificed throughout the years for our family and has shown me the type of man I want to be — patient, kind, fearless and always ready to put family before anything else.

And in memory of my cousins, Nicholas Murray and Tanya Murray and J.R. Murrary, who loved life and left behind families who will always love them because love never dies.

Acknowledgments

I would like to personally acknowledge several people who have made this possibly through either direct or indirect involvement.

Geofrrey Ronning, Sean Michael Andrews, John Cebrone, Richard Nongard, K.C. Johnson, Nathan Thomas, and the many other hypnotists who have contributed to my knowledge of hypnosis.

I would also like to acknowledge my good friend Helen Paulus, whose guidance and programs have helped me achieve so much more than I thought possible.

And of course, I have to acknowledge my parents, John and Diane, and my brothers and sisters, David, Tammy, Melody, Carl and Sam for always supporting me and being there for me.

Foreword

It's been said that we only use a fraction of our brain's capability. And yet, as much as science has learned about the physical make-up of the brain, the "mind" remains somewhat of a mystery.

Most people don't understand the difference between the conscious mind and the unconscious, or subconscious, mind. And in not understanding the unconscious mind, they become slaves to behavior patterns that have formed at an unconscious level.

This book teaches the basic fundamentals of hypnosis, a way to tap into the unconscious mind and make real changes in our behavior.

Table of Contents

1

Introduction

I want to thank you for your interest in hypnosis. The practice of hypnosis can be complex or simple and can be used in a variety of applications. I hope that you find hypnosis to be as fascinating and useful as I do. Every year through hypnotic shows and corporate seminars I introduce thousands of people to the power of hypnosis, and I am happy to have you join me on this journey today.

It is my desire in this book to reveal to you how you can take control of your life and achieve your goals with remarkable ease using hypnosis. This book will guide you to higher personal and professional satisfaction while revealing the power of hypnosis.

I know these are strong claims. Coming from a skeptical and scientific background I would hesitate to even suggest such benefits, but the data is irrefutable.

In the Introduction of this book it may be too early for me to tell you that your life may never be the same – but it will not.

You alone hold the control and power of your mind. You see, with hypnosis as your tool, you have the ability to tap into the power of your mind, to control your destiny and enrich your life and the lives of others.

This tool does not take a lot of time, nor is it expensive. It only requires a small investment of your energy and willingness to experience its usefulness. Nothing more.

Hypnosis is a gift. My goal is to teach you how to use this gift in a way that will positively influence your life. You can make healthy physical and mental changes to yourself to become the person you want to be.

Only you can change your attitudes to become a better person. Continuous improvement is not something that just happens – just like anything else; you have to put effort into working on it.

You, and those around you, will be happy that you invested time in yourself. May you enjoy the journey as much as the destination.

I'll see you on the path.

2

What Hypnosis Is – And Is Not

Most people are conditioned by movies and television to think hypnosis is an evil tool that is used by scowling, menacing figures who live in the shadows. This shady character is a far cry from the professional hypnotist. Negative portrayals degrade the value of the state of hypnosis and spread misinformation.

In fact, hypnosis is a natural state of mind that all of us experience every single day. Have you ever found yourself engaged by a project that focused all your attention on the task at hand, and the time seemed to fly by? Have you ever tried to speak with somebody who was working behind a computer keyboard and you had trouble getting his or her attention?

These scenarios describe a natural state of hypnosis, which is also called a natural hypnotic trance. A natural hypnotic trance is a state of mind where intense focus eliminates distractions from the external world, and your internal world expands. The door to your subconscious opens wide.

Another common state of hypnosis in our day-to-day lives is daydreams. How often have you "spaced out" and found yourself not using your conscious mind at all – simply thinking of nothing?

Most researchers are now in agreement on the definition of hypnosis:

Any person who is willing to be hypnotized can experience hypnosis. The only requirements needed for self-hypnosis are the knowledge of basic methods and the desire to do it.

Hypnosis is…

the state of mind that provides you with the ability to follow suggestion without conscious intent.

There are traits that can identify if a person has reached a state of hypnosis. Look for these characteristics in yourself or someone who is being hypnotized:

- A reduction of inhibitions
- Complete physical relaxation
- Focused concentration on what is being said
- Mental and emotional dormancy
- Fluttering rapid movements of the eyes
- Concentrated awareness of the senses (taste, touch, feel, smell, and hearing)
- Stationary, still body position

What does hypnosis do? Hypnosis is a tool that is used to help people reach their goals. It is not a cure-all that can be administered once and never revisited. Hypnosis is useful and highly effective when applied for subconscious issues such as weight gain, stress, insomnia, pain, and shyness.

There are dozens of uses for hypnosis.

As mentioned earlier, the definition of hypnosis is the quieting of the conscious mind to allow access to the powerful subconscious mind. The process of hypnosis is a natural state that involves complete relaxation and passivity.

The activation of the subconscious mind allows suggestions to be made easily without passing through the judgment of the conscious mind.

Why Does Hypnosis Work?

Hypnosis uses the power of suggestion to influence the subconscious mind. Tapping into the subconscious provides lasting results in a person's exhibited behaviors.

The subconscious mind is the primary influence on a person's attitudes, beliefs, and behavior. Hypnosis is the tool that can be used to reprogram the subconscious to make lasting changes to undesirable behaviors and thought patterns that are evident in the conscious mind.

Hypnosis is used to change your fundamental beliefs in the way in which you view yourself and others, and the underlying reasons why you feel and act the way you do.

The brain is like a tape recorder. Your thoughts are like recordings in your mind. The thoughts that you have throughout every day are really just the recordings being played back. Once your mind is programmed to think a certain way, then that is how you think. If this way of thought is hindering you from living up to your full potential, then you can benefit from hypnosis.

Hypnosis is used to reprogram old thoughts and beliefs to give you more desirable behaviors and attitudes.

Hypnosis is all about specifics – a general statement like "I want to be a better person" won't work. Pinpointing specifically which behavior you want to change is necessary in effective hypnotherapy.

In order to fully understand how hypnosis works, it is important to discuss the mechanics of your conscious and subconscious state.

Each day we fluctuate between the conscious and subconscious state of mind. Almost all of our activities are performed subconsciously!

When activities are performed subconsciously, there is no decision-making process that takes place - no consideration of the outcome is thought out. The activity is simply performed. Conversely, when activities occur on a conscious level, there is often resistance, reluctance and the opportunity to discard the activity.

Here is an example:

If I'm a smoker then I don't say to myself: "a cigarette sounds really good, I will have one in ten minutes." I simply pick up a cigarette and light up without any consideration.

It's a habit that is done on a subconscious level.

Now, here is a workplace example to consider:

If I'm in the habit (again, an unconscious behavior) of not getting any work done for the first thirty minutes of my shift, I am exhibiting unproductive behavior. Instead of getting right to work, I have a routine of visiting co-workers, clearing my desk, getting coffee, surfing the Internet, or other inefficient activities. For me to consciously address this issue would be difficult, if not impossible. In my mind, I would form numerous reasons to support the wasteful, inefficient behavior. This is because my habit runs deep into my subconscious mind and can only be fundamentally changed through focused work on the subconscious – also known as hypnosis.

If I changed the behavior at a subconscious level, there wouldn't be any resistance because activities that occur at a subconscious level occur without consideration or effort!

They simply happen and you automatically adopt what is programmed subconsciously on a conscious level.

Recall the last time you operated your vehicle. Perhaps it was while you were going to work, shopping, or to the doctor's office. Think about that trip. Do you recall the details of that drive? I doubt it. Most people do not consciously drive their vehicles.

For most people driving is something done in our unconscious mind. You don't say to yourself, "I must put the vehicle in gear, release the parking brake, check over my shoulder for oncoming traffic, signal to turn left, release the steering wheel to right the vehicle and stay in this lane."

Driving is typically done subconsciously. Your subconscious is aware of everything that is happening but consciously you're thinking about errands you need to do, television shows you want to watch later that evening, or things you wished you would have said or done throughout the day.

We tend to multitask, all day long. We operate on both levels and easily and naturally move between the conscious and the subconscious.

Take this simple test:

I fly a
a kite everyday

What did you see? Your selective consciousness would probably have you focus on just the letters in the sentence structure. I'm certain you also saw the book you're holding; perhaps you saw your hands or some of your fingers, possibly the floor beneath the book, and maybe the surrounding furniture. But although you saw these things, your mind didn't direct you to pay conscious attention to them.

Consciously, you automatically became very selective of what you were processing. Subconsciously your awareness was fully engaged by all these other factors.

In addition there are certainly other factors involved as well. Perhaps once directed consciously you will become aware of the sounds in the background, the temperature of your surroundings, the contact your body is making with the furniture, or the contact your feet are making with the floor.

More than likely while taking the test, those items were not in your consciousness. You may have also missed the repeated letter "a".

Sometimes during stress control seminars people say, "I have so much to juggle that it is hard for me to stay focused. I end up not getting anything accomplished because I can't seem to stay on track to reach my priorities."

Do you ever feel this way? Have you ever had an issue you could not resolve? Have you ever found yourself trying to remember the answer to a question that you were certain you knew, but could not recall? Your conscious mind blocked the retrieval of this bit of information.

Everyone at some point in their lives has found themselves struggling to remember someone's name. As soon as you stopped trying to remember the name, it probably came to you. Maybe you awoke in the morning with it, or maybe as soon as you consciously directed your attention to other things, your subconscious took over and delivered that information to you.

The other day I was watching a program on musical artists. The show featured interviews with some of the most popular and influential songwriters in the world today, and their experience writing songs. One songwriter told a story about waking in the middle of the night to jot down an inspiration.

He wrote a song subconsciously and it wasn't until morning when he found the song sitting beside his bed. It became the biggest hit of his career. The phrase "the harder you think about it, the easier it is to forget" is certainly true.

In fact, if you are ever struggling to remember something simply tell yourself these specific words:

"I don't know how quickly that answer will come to me, but until it does I will direct my attention to a different task."

You will find that missing piece of data is quickly delivered to you. Your subconscious is always working. Embrace it and it will work wonders for you.

Why does this work so well? Well, we are "presupposing" an outcome or giving ourselves a suggestion that the information will be forthcoming.

Ten Common Questions Answered

People often have questions when first learning about hypnosis. Even if you know a bit about hypnosis and its benefits, you may still have areas where you have questions.

The following are ten of the most commonly asked questions, and their answers.

1. What's the difference between hypnosis and hypnotherapy?

The practice of improving the quality of life and healing through a relaxed, rested state where the subconscious mind is receptive to external suggestions is called hypnotherapy.

Hypnosis allows us to place suggestions directly into the subconscious mind, and what takes hold in the subconscious is automatically acted on by the conscious mind.

The relaxed, sleep-like state is considered hypnosis.

2. How is self-hypnosis different than hypnosis?

They are actually the same thing since the state of mind is self-produced even when working with a hypnotist. The difference is that self-hypnosis is self-managed and guided, while standard hypnosis is guided by a hypnotist.

3. Who makes the best hypnosis candidates?

The best hypnotic subjects tend to be people that are intelligent, have the ability to visualize freely, are creatively inclined, and are able to freely express their emotions.

4. Who has trouble being hypnotized?

People that are too critical, overanalyze things, have a low mental visualization ability, cannot focus or pay attention for an extended period of time, are of lower than- average intelligence, or are overly inhibited tend to have difficulty removing the conscious barrier to allow themselves to be hypnotized.

5. Can I see the difference between my conscious and subconscious minds?

Sure you can, you use both everyday! Examples of the use of the conscious mind are when you are engaged in conversation with someone else, you are working out an analytical problem, or you are pricing out the best deal at the grocery store. Conversely, the subconscious mind is in use when you are daydreaming about a memory, are truly relaxing, or right before falling asleep.

6. Is there anything I need to do before trying self-hypnosis?

It is important that anyone trying to use self-hypnosis to change a core issue have a high level of self-awareness.

You will need to recognize when deeper issues are involved that are beyond your capability to handle, and seek appropriate care and assistance.

You will also need to be willing and able to let go of an old belief system that is getting in the way. The removal and replacement of belief systems is the mark of a successful self-hypnosis endeavor.

7. Can you explain the subconscious?

The subconscious mind is everything except for the conscious thoughts. Obviously, that encompasses a lot! It is not one region of the brain; rather it is continuously changing as the conscious thoughts in your mind change.

An example of a subconscious activity is your breath. It occurs throughout your life, although you are rarely breathing consciously. Now that I have brought it up here in this paragraph, you are probably thinking about it, thus bringing your breathing in the conscious mind. As you continue reading and something else comes into your conscious mind, your breath with go back to being a subconscious activity. This is the organic flow of activity between the conscious and subconscious minds.

8. Can you trust your subconscious mind?

People sometimes fear their subconscious. They are often afraid that they will revert to back to some undesirable behavior. They often fear the unknown. The subconscious mind is where you can gain a deeper understanding of your core self. The subconscious is something that can be shaped and formed to become the best you can be.

It's important to remember that you won't do anything with your subconscious that you don't want to have done to it. Working with the subconscious through hypnosis is not voodoo. You choose what you act upon and what you don't.

Your opinions and beliefs about this question will reveal whether or not you will have initial success with hypnosis. If you find you have reservations about accessing the subconscious intentionally, work through those negative thoughts first when planning your hypnosis work.

9. Can I change my character with hypnosis?

People with a high level of self-awareness often wonder if the less desirable thoughts and values are character flaws, and if they can be changed through hypnosis.

Character is said to be largely genetic, which means a person is born with certain character tendencies. However, it is also believed that a character is develop and shaped by a person's upbringing.

Hypnosis can be used to take control over any genetic character predispositions. You can do significant work with the subconscious mind to reprogram your thought, belief, and value systems.

10. Is hypnosis applicable in the business world?

It sure is! Most of what we do at work involves the subconscious mind on some level. Hypnosis can be used for all levels within the organization from the top leaders down to the front line staff.

Here are some scenarios of when hypnosis could be used in the corporate world.

If you supervise staff, you have probably at some point in your career run into one of these problems:

- You have a team that is not function properly and don't know what to do.
- You find yourself having preconceived opinions about an employee and you don't know why.
- You can never seem to get everything done in the day.

- You can't seem to get ahead to the next step in your career.

As you can see, hypnosis can be used to varying degrees in many different applications. There is no reason to fear hypnosis. It is a harmless way to make lasting, positive changes.

Hypnotic Myths & Misconceptions

Some people erroneously believe that in order to be hypnotized you must be weak-willed. Numerous studies have shown hypnotizability is completely unrelated to that personality characteristic. Hypnotizability has nothing to do with gullibility, submissiveness, imagination or being weak-willed.

Some people believe that in order to be hypnotized you must try or put forth effort. The studies and my own experiences have shown this is not accurate.

Most hypnotized people say, "It just happened." Or if I'm working with a pain client they may say, "I immediately felt no pain," or if they are overcoming a fear of public speaking they will tell me, "I felt comfortable, confident, and relaxed and I had absolutely no fears regarding the process."

If a client is working with me to improve their career they may say, "I adopted a failure-free attitude and found myself being dramatically more productive."

In fact, oftentimes if people are having trouble experiencing hypnosis it is because they are trying too hard. When they relax and try less, hypnosis happens!

In the past, hypnosis has been viewed as fake or dangerous. Neither could be farther from the truth. Hypnosis is a mental state of consciousness that is naturally induced because the participant sets aside willpower and the conscious mind to allow himself to be hypnotized. This openness and willingness to be hypnotized is the reason why hypnosis works.

People often worry that they will lose control if they are hypnotized. The opposite is actually true. A series of hypnosis sessions will allow the subject to gain more control over their life and actions.

What Does it Feel Like to Be Hypnotized?

Being hypnotized is really a state of heightened consciousness. A common myth is that you will actually lose consciousness – that simply is not true!

You will be much more aware then before. This is because of your highly focused concentration and relaxed state.

After the first hypnosis session, participants often say the hypnotic induction was much different than they expected. Pre-established opinions of hypnosis make subjects think it is much more extreme and intense than it actually is. It is common for people to think that they have not actually been hypnotized at all, when in fact they have.

Many first-timers say that they hear every word and experience a complete relaxation unlike anything achievable without hypnosis. It may take several hypnosis sessions for a subject to equate this feeling of comfort and relaxation with hypnosis.

After several sessions a subject is able to get to deeper levels of hypnosis. Deep levels of hypnosis are best for making fundamental changes to your beliefs.

Sometimes, at very deep levels of hypnosis, subjects experience something called catalepsy. This only occurs when a subject is in a deep trance. Catalepsy is a response where the subject is unable to move their body during hypnosis. Don't be afraid that this will happen to you involuntarily. Everything that happens during hypnosis is because you want it to happen. If it is your belief that you will be in control during the entire session, and maintain awareness, you will.

How Hypnotism Works

There is a fairly standard process for hypnosis. It involves:

• Induction - This is used to induce hypnosis in a subject.

• Deepening – This creates a higher level of concentration in the subject and helps them focus more deeply.

• Suggestions – Here's where the "seed" is planted for change in the subject's subconscious. Suggestions are used to help them work through the desired changes in the subconscious.

• Awakening – A planned process that allows the subject to awaken comfortably.

The following is a detailed step-by-step description of how the hypnosis process works, along with some examples of techniques that are most commonly used to achieve results. These are the steps to successful and meaningful hypnosis.

Step 1:

Achieve a light alpha state through induction exercises. The early hypnotic state involves alpha brainwaves. Achieving a light alpha state is done in a variety of ways. When this point is reached, you will feel a shift in consciousness. It doesn't really matter how the light alpha state is achieved as long as the subject feels relaxed and calm, and is receptive to hypnosis. For many people, simply resting the body and closing the eyes, then taking a series of deep cleansing breaths is enough.

There are several widely accepted induction exercises. Some of the most common hypnosis induction techniques are:

- Breathing countdown
- Fractional relaxation (also known as "progressive relaxation")
- Visual fixation on a fixed point
- Arm dropping
- Counting stairs on a visualized staircase
- Hand raising

Step 2:

Deepen the alpha state.

Again, techniques vary for methods to create a deeper alpha state and help the mind focus. Induction and deepening techniques include guided journeys or fractional relaxation to aid in mental concentration.

Suggestions are the main strategy of fractional relaxation. Each area of the body is focused on separately, and the technique often starts at the top of the head and works down the body all the way to the toes.

Fractional relaxation does several things. First, the fractional relaxation method of induction helps the subject feel more relaxed. Secondly, it also helps deepen the hypnosis, moving slowly from the conscious mind to the subconscious mind.

Fractional relaxation is useful because it makes the subject aware of the process of relaxing and removes external stimuli. And lastly, the conscious mind moves from the primary role to the secondary, and the subconscious mind becomes accessible. This accessibility is necessary to make real change to the subconscious mind.

A guided journey involves visualization in order to focus the subject's subconscious mind. Scripts are often used by the guide in cases where a hypnotist is used to guide hypnosis.

In the case of a self-hypnosis subject, guided journeys and visualization is often accomplished with an audio recording of a visualization exercise.

Other deepening techniques include:

• A countdown with synchronized relaxation breathing.

• Purposeful quiet time when you allow yourself to reach a state of hypnotic induction on your own.

• Visualization of pleasant places that invoke positive senses.

Step 3:

Making changes to a person's subconscious mind using suggestions.

Once the subconscious mind has been brought to the forefront, it is ready for suggestions and visualizations that will be used to reprogram attitudes and unproductive beliefs.

These attitudes and beliefs are directly linked to the change we are trying to make.

Suggestions and visualizations are used to communicate with the subconscious mind.

The first step in making changes to the subconscious is removing the old belief systems that are hindering positive changes in the person's life. The old belief systems are most likely causing the problematic behavior, and must be let go because they will get in the way of any real changes.

It is not an option to simply create a new belief system on top of an old one, either. This will give conflicted results in behaviors because inside the subconscious mind, the belief systems in place are conflicted. The goal of this phase of hypnosis is to create a balance and alignment between the fundamental belief system in the subconscious mind, and the wants and needs of the conscious mind. Once this has been done properly, we can influence the subconscious mind to create a new, desired behavior.

We'll talk more about suggestions, visualization, and other way to change the subconscious through hypnosis later in this book.

Hypnosis works in three simple ways:

1. Cleansing breaths create relaxation.

2. Calm and still relaxation creates a mind ready for suggestion.

3. And a mind ready for suggestion is essential for effective hypnosis.

Step 4:

Awaken properly.

A subject can be effectively awakened by simply suggesting waking up. You could also try guiding a gentler, gradual arousal that will leave the subject feeling great.

For example the hypnotist can suggest that the subject slowly wakes up feeling refreshed. The awakening process is a formal one, and marks the transition back to regular consciousness from a hypnotic state.

There are principles to hypnosis that you should understand so that you realize the relationship between exhibited behavior and these basic hypnosis principles.

• The Reversed Effect Rule

This rule does what it says. The more a hypnotist tries to change a behavior, the more difficult it is to change. If there is a conflict between the conscious mind and subconscious mind, this conflict causes the subject to do the opposite of what is suggested. This is similar to when a child is told to do something they don't want to do – they often tend to do the opposite.

How would you see the Reversed Effect Rule? Remember the last time you tried to remember an important name or bit of information but you couldn't recall it? The harder you tried, the harder it became. You may have thought to yourself, "I'll probably remember it at 2:00 AM, or in the shower, etc." And it's often true – when you are relaxed and thinking of something else, you will effortlessly be able to remember the information.

• Each thought created in your mind creates some sort of a response in the body.

If an idea has a strong emotional link it will produce a response in the body. This principle is so valuable because even disease and sickness in the body can be hindered by thoughts and attitudes.

This response principle is witnessed through a person's negative responses to situations. The way to change this is to view a person's situation through positive attitude lenses. By changing the negative views into a positive attitude through hypnosis, you are giving power to you mind and changing your mindset for a better life.

• Realization of goals comes from suggestions that are imagined or expected.

This means that if the subconscious senses there is a goal (or is even told flat out that there is a goal), a subject will subconsciously try to reach the goal. A subject that knows what it is working toward will help produce conscious behaviors that support the achievement of the goal.

• Visualization can be used to create new habits.

By acting out an imagined activity during hypnosis, a pattern of behavior can be changed to mimic the new, imagined behavior.

• A suggestion with strong emotion tied to it is dominant.

A suggestion is made stronger when a strong emotion is connected to it. Previous, non-emotional suggestions will be replaced by new, emotionally-powerful suggestions.

3

The Science of Hypnosis

In the laboratory setting, researchers have studied hypnosis to learn more about its positive effects. In the early studies regarding hypnosis, some unethical psychological researchers used hypnosis inappropriately to create false memories, hallucinations, compulsions and alternate behavior in people so that they could be studied and analyzed.

Experimentation is no longer conducted in such a haphazard manner. The mind is a powerful thing. Misconduct and abuse of the role of hypnotist are taken very seriously in the world of psychology today.

Today's researches pay close attention to using hypnosis as a device for psychological repair, as well as a part of their scientific research. Hypnosis is used to improve lives and learn more about the way the conscious and subconscious minds work together.

The Mind-Body Connection

One of the medical tools that is used to study the hypnotic state is called a Positron Emission Tomography (PET) scan. It records an image of the brain during the brain's thought process. It has been found that hypnosis produces a very specific pattern of activity within the brain. It shows an increased blood flow in the right anterior cingulate cortex, which suggests that there is an internal focus. This brain activity is very different from normal and waking states.

Let's examine brain wave activities.

There are four types of brain wave classifications.

They are:

- Beta

- Alpha

- Theta

- Delta

Beta waves are the normal waking consciousness state. As you read this book, you are in beta. Beta is a state where you are wide-awake and aware of your surroundings.

How do you get to beta? Simply wake up and start moving around and taking in stimuli. Begin actively thinking and get engaged to use beta brainwaves.

Alpha waves are slower patterns that are found when people relax, listen to music, or meditate. To utilize alpha brainwaves, close your eyes and take deep breaths. Focus on relaxing. This is the early stages of hypnosis and visualization.

Theta waves are present just before and after you awaken from deep sleep. They are also present during the hypnotized trance state.

How can you reach theta brainwave activity? This state of mind is achieved during light sleep, deep meditation, memory, or meditation. A guided meditation (either with a hypnotist or a self-hypnosis soundtrack) will take you to your innermost subconscious mind.

Delta waves are deep sleep. Delta allows you to rejuvenate and dream. You can get to delta brainwaves through falling fast asleep.

The alpha and sometimes theta brainwaves are used during hypnosis.

Using the PET scan, scientists have made some exciting discoveries regarding hypnosis. For instance, some people have tried to suggest that hypnosis is simply active imagination. This has now been proven to not be the case.

Using the PET scan, researchers have discovered different regions of the brain are utilized during hypnosis. These regions differ from the regions of the brain exercised while using imagination. That means when a person imagines a sound, the activity is located in a different part in the brain.

When that same person experiences a hypnotic hallucination, the brain activity is recorded in an entirely different area.

Henry Szechtman of McMaster University in Hamilton, Ontario conducted a study that used a PET scan to record the brain activity of individuals who imagined a scene, and then experienced a similar hypnotic hallucination created through hypnotizing the subjects and providing them with a suggestion to experience the hallucination.

It has been determined there is absolutely no relationship between hypnosis and imagination.

Researchers found that auditory hallucination and imagining a sound are both generated within each of us. However the hallucination in hypnosis, like that of real hearing, is experienced as being received from an outside source.

Researchers then tried to isolate the area of the brain responsible for the different brain response pattern while in hypnosis. Eight subjects were studied by the University during this amazing session.

During the session, each person heard the exact same audio track while the PET scan recorded the brain activity.

The brain activity was studied during four different circumstances:

1. While they were listening in their normal waking state.

2. While they rested and listened to the audio track.

3. While they just imagined hearing the audio track.

4. While they were in a hypnotized state responding to a suggestion to hallucinate the audio track, although it was not actually playing.

The research revealed the region of the brain called the right anterior cingulate cortex was just as active while the volunteers were hallucinating as it was while they were actually hearing the track.

In comparison, the right anterior cingulate cortex was not active at all while the volunteers were imagining they heard the audio. Clearly something tangible is going on!

The Stanford Hypnotic Susceptibility Scales

These scales were developed in the late 1950's by Stanford University psychologists Andrea M. Weitzenhoffer and Ernest R. Hilgard. They are used to determine the extent to which a subject responds to the hypnotic state.

For instance, one model of the Stanford scales consists of a series of twelve actions which test the depth of the hypnotic state. Such a test includes the suggestion that a subject's arm is getting heavier and will lower slowly as the weight increases and pushes their arm down towards the floor.

In other words, hypnotic suggestion has completely deceived the right anterior cingulate cortex area of the brain into registering the hallucinated audio as genuine.

another test, ammonia is passed under a subject's nose after the suggestion is given that they have no sense of smell.

If the subject responds appropriately, then a positive score is awarded. If the subject's hand does not move or the subject reacts to the ammonia smell, they are not as suggestible.

Scores range from zero, for those that do not respond to any of the hypnotic suggestions, to twelve, for those individuals that respond positively to all of them. As you can imagine, most people score in the middle. Researchers have determined that a person's ability to respond to hypnosis remains consistent throughout their life.

They established this by testing individuals over the course of 10, 15, and 25 years. It was found that individuals maintained the approximate same score as previously tested.

It is interesting to note that the study also has provided evidence that hypnotic suggestibility has some hereditary components as well. For instance, identical twins are more likely than same sex fraternal twins to share Stanford scale characteristics.

It is important to note that a lower score on the Stanford scale does not mean that one cannot by hypnotized. What it communicates is that the induction will take longer and getting to a trance state will be a different process than with a higher-scored individual.

Conducting Your Own Suggestibility Testing

The suggestibility tests are used to gauge how receptive to hypnosis a subject will be. In the case of self-hypnosis you can do this to yourself. If you are hypnotizing someone else, you can use it a suggestibility test on someone else.

The benefit of a suggestibility test is for the hypnotist. There

is really nothing that comes out of it for the subject being hypnotized. The exercises provide information that is used by the hypnotist to create the most efficient and effective hypnosis experience for the subject.

With that said, even though the suggestibility tests are not designed for the subject's benefit, there is something in it for them. The subject will be convinced and it will help them focus on the fact that they are indeed being hypnotized. This "prep time" helps get them ready for the real hypnosis session.

Charles Tebbetts, a renowned hypnosis research and pioneer, created several suggestibility tests that are still in use today. His methods were often a combination of other researcher's techniques, so the exact origin of this one is not known for certain.

Magnetic Hands Suggestibility Test

Step 1:

Have the subject hold out both arms at a 90 degree angle in front of them, fully extended with the palms facing each other.

Step 2:

Move the subject's hands from about three feet apart to about two feet apart. Then place your index finger in the space about halfway between the hands.

Step 3:

Tell the subject to focus on your finger. Then you should count backwards from three to one. Tell the subject to shut their eyes when you reach one.

Step 4:

Tell them the point of this exercise - to keep their eyes pointed in the same position as they were when their eyes were opened, staring at your finger.

Step 5:

Tell the subject to visualize that you have a magnet and are placing it in the palm of one of their hands. Touch them like you are actually doing this.

Step 6:

Tell them you have another magnet, one with the opposite pole, which you are placing in their other hand. Touch them as if you are actually doing this.

Step 7:

Ask the subject to visualize that the magnets are being drawn toward each other. Closer and closer the magnets become. Tell the subject to feel the magnets pulling toward one another. Then tell the subject that when they touch they should let the magnets fall and open their eyes.

Inevitably the subject's hands will touch. You now know that you have a candidate that is susceptible to the benefits of hypnosis. Even if this exercise doesn't work for your subject (or you) – don't worry. It just means you need to try different induction techniques until you find one that works well.

Effective Suggestion Structuring

Effective suggestions are the key to removing unwanted behavior patterns or getting pre-planned desired results from hypnosis. However, for a hypnosis session to be effective and target the appropriate habits, you must have well constructed suggestions.

Self-hypnosis requires you to create well-worded suggestions prior to your session with careful thought. To maximize effectiveness you will need to create a linkage to your goals and objectives. The professional hypnotist will do the work of creating suggestions for you, based on your desired outcomes. An experienced hypnotist is best because you will also benefit from their years of client experience with effective suggestions.

Follow these tips for writing the best suggestions that will work for you. Remember, suggestions are really just instructions for the subconscious mind.

DO…..keep it positive.

Your suggestions need to be kept in a positive mindset because the subconscious mind is more likely to be receptive to suggestions that are positively worded. For example, a positive suggestion like "I am sleeping more every day" is more effective than its negative counterpart of "I am not an insomniac."

DON'T…..just say each suggestion only one time.

Repetition is important. It's okay if some suggestions are only used one time, but as a general rule, it's important to repeatedly say each suggestion so that the subconscious hears it a few times to get the point across.

DO…..customize the instructions so they lead up to your goals during hypnosis.

The actual wording needs to say "I" and not "you." This is so your subconscious can identify with what you are saying.

You have to talk to yourself in the first person for the message to be heard.

DON'T…..jump all over the place with the sequencing of your suggestions.

It's important to put your suggestions in order so that you are steadily improving upon each instruction you are giving your subconscious mind, leading up to your overall goal.

DO…..be specific.

Just saying "I will stop smoking" won't work. You need to be specific with your timeframe and what the actual result will be. For example, you can say something like, "I am steadily going to reduce the number of cigarettes I smoke by one a day until I reach my goal of zero cigarettes per day."

DON'T…..use just suggestions alone.

The best success comes to those who use a multi-faceted approach to hypnosis. Include visualizations and emotion oriented words along with suggestions to help your subconscious mind to absorb what you are saying.

Visualizations are technically suggestions anyway, so a vivid image that you can portray is more effective to the subconscious. Try words like "beautiful", "enthralling", "perfect", and "exciting" to get your mind to respond to your goals.

DO…..keep it simple.

Suggestions need to be clear and concise. Use short chunks with one idea per suggestion – it's the best way to work with the subconscious mind.

Also keep everything in the simple-to-understand present tense, whenever possible. Never use the present progressive form of verbs. That means avoid conjugations like "I am trying…" and use the straight present tense of verbs in your suggestions.

4

The Many Personal Benefits of Hypnosis

Hypnosis can help you to make the personal changes you desire. There are four critical areas in which hypnosis can help you improve the quality of your life. They are:

1. Psychological

2. Physical

3. Chemical

4. Emotional

These simple classifications quickly take on enormous proportions when you begin to consider the territory covered by each. While we don't have the space to cover all these areas within this book, we will cover the most common.

The personal benefits of hypnosis are most evident through the behavioral change it helps instill.

Psychological Changes through Hypnosis

What changes would you like to make to your personality?

What behaviors and fundamental beliefs would you like changed?

Here are just a few areas you can address with hypnosis:

• Motivation

• Confidence

• Attitude

• Creativity

• Goal Focus

• Stress Level

In fact, specific behavioral-change hypnosis is the most popular application of hypnotic techniques.

Many people have a desire to change a behavioral aspect of their life and find it difficult, if not impossible. Most people make behavioral changes based on self-discipline and willpower. The problem is that this is an inefficient and ineffective way to facilitate long-term significant change.

Let's consider some of the more common specific behavior change applications of hypnosis.

Weight Loss

I know many people who have tried to lose weight repeatedly before using hypnosis. Once they began to properly apply hypnosis, the weight loss was successful. The research supports this success pattern. My own weight loss hypnotic audio program has led many people to their own success with weight loss.

In addition, numerous experiments have been done by magazine, newspapers, and television shows that have tested hypnosis as a suitable weight loss technique.

In this section of this book, you will witness an in-depth explanation of how hypnosis works in making behavior changes. Weight loss is an easy example to use to explain to the new hypnosis subject how and why the hypnosis process works. Let's get started.

A weight loss candidate should practice two basic behaviors to successfully lose weight using hypnosis as their primary tool. Consider adding these to your weight loss plan:

1. Keep a food journal that accounts for everything that you plan to eat throughout the course of the day.

Include the calorie content of each item and total the day's calories in advance of eating them.

2. Listen to a hypnotic weight loss audio program daily until you have reached your desired weight loss goals.

When losing weight through hypnosis, there are several important points that you will need to keep in mind in order to reach your desired weight in a healthy manner. It is essential that you pay attention to these factors so that you can accomplish and maintain your weight loss over time.

When using hypnosis to lose weight, be sure to:

• Practice the food journaling process.

Keeping track of your dietary intake is designed to create awareness about the subconscious eating that you do. Research has recently determined that maintaining a food journal daily is the number one way to maintain weight loss over time.

• Be certain to eat at least 1,200 calories per day.

Reducing your calorie intake below this level can be hazardous to your health. Plus, while you may initially lose weight, as soon as you return to a higher calorie level the weight will pile back on. The extreme calorie reduction is too great of a shock to your metabolism.

• Avoid crash dieting by not losing weight too quickly.

If you plan to lose one to two pounds per week by watching what you eat and using the hypnosis recordings to support your behavioral and physical responses, you will be able to sustain long term weight loss. If, one the other hand, you lose large amounts of weight quickly, you will have a greater chance of gaining it back.

Using hypnosis for weight loss should be viewed as an ongoing process, not one that is a permanent fix forever. If you continue to work on yourself using hypnosis and conscious planned eating, you will have a great chance for sustained success.

There are several steps associated with understanding weight loss. To properly use hypnosis as a weight loss tool, you will need to understand several behaviors you exhibit when it comes to food. Ask yourself these questions:

1. What are the places and times that trigger me to overeat?

2. Why do non-hypnosis weight loss plans fail?

3. What emotions cause me to eat when I'm not hungry?

4. What learned subconscious behaviors have I acquired throughout my lifetime?

To get the most from your weight loss hypnosis experience try the following. First, spend some time answering the four questions above. In a moment, we will discuss exactly how the answers to these four points link to your hypnosis results. Then, learn about the mind's response to suggestions and hypnotic commands – and use this learning to plan out your own ways to get around the anti-suggestive wall of the mind. That is your conscious mind getting in the way of your weight loss goals.

Weight loss, no matter if it is assisted by hypnotherapy or practiced alone, always involves eating fewer calories than you burn. There are days where the body will retain water weight, but that is not fat weight, and it will go away.

Hypnosis is an effective weight loss tool because when used correctly, it works on the root of the weight problem.

What are the roots of why you have trouble losing weight?

And how exactly will hypnosis be used to deal with these issues subconsciously? First you will need to look at why you have weight issues to begin with.

Why do you eat? Often it is not because you are hungry; rather it's for other reasons. As a small child, many of us were taught unhealthy reasons to eat. Often when a child cries, the caregiver stops the crying by offering a bottle, cookie, or other food. This is done because the caregiver is not sure why the child is crying, and assumes it is out of hunger.

In reality, small children cry for many different reasons like wanting love, wanting comfort, or wanting to be held. When you were given food to stop you from feeling a negative emotion, you subconsciously were taught that food is used for comfort, in place of love, as an emotional crutch for dealing with fear – any emotional need you can think of!

Food is often also used as a reward. If you were good as a child, were you ever rewarded with a cookie or piece of candy? This reward system is subconsciously carried forward in life to adulthood, where many of us subconsciously reward ourselves with food. Did you work especially hard on a project at work and stay late? Getting a pizza and having ice cream for dessert is your reward to yourself. This unhealthy relationship with food is rarely consciously planned, so therefore this way of thought needs to be reprogrammed in the mind using hypnosis.

The subconscious programming many of us have as children carries through to adulthood. This is why most traditional non-hypnosis weight loss plans fail. Traditional non-hypnosis weight loss plans do not include working with the unconscious mind. They typically use affirmations in the conscious mind to promote healthy eating. This really only works well in people without any subconscious issues related to food – which is rare.

So, how do you "un-program" yourself to no longer subconsciously think this way? That's where hypnosis comes in.

The patterns in the way you think about yourself have to be in line with the suggestions that are being made from you or someone else. If there is a separation between the suggestions and your own pattern of thinking, your mind will ignore the suggestions completely. In order to change a thought pattern in the mind, the negative patterns should be handled first, and the belief patterns should also be reworked to create new patterns and beliefs in their place. Only then can you begin to use new positive suggestions to really impact your weight loss goals.

The process of reworking old thought patterns and beliefs regarding food and inserting new, healthy ones in their place involves several steps.

Step 1:

Identify what you want to change about where you eat.

Ask yourself the following questions:

• Do you eat in front of the TV, in the car, or in the bed?

• Do you eat more at work than at home?

Step 2:

Identify what you want to change about when you eat.

Ask yourself the following question:

What type of eater are you emotionally – do you eat because you are bored, tired, feel unappreciated, happy, sad, lonely, depressed, have low self-esteem, etc.?

Step 3:

Find something better to do than eat.

Considering your answers to the questions above, list at least five things you would rather do than eat.

1.

2.

3.

4.

5.

Step 4:

Replace unnecessary eating with other behaviors.

You have now identified the specific situations in your eating habits that you want to change, and behaviors that you will use to replace unnecessary eating in your life.

For example, perhaps you find yourself eating in front of the TV, and you would like to change that behavior. Next imagine that you prefer to drink ice water rather than eat in front of the TV. This is one example of a behavioral change that can be made through hypnosis.

Another example is this – imagine that you would like to change the fact that you eat when you are bored. Next picture that you prefer to talk on the phone instead of eating food. This change can be made through hypnosis.

The process is simply identifying the root behaviors that are causing you to be overweight, and then creating a new physical response to the triggers that cause you to overeat.

The last step is to create suggestions that will be used to help you communicate with your subconscious mind.

Now you know that you will need to do more than just tell yourself to change behavior or use affirmations. Self-talk and affirmations may work for the first few days, but after a small bit of time, you will most likely revert back to the old behavior because you never reprogrammed your subconscious.

The way to make lasting change through hypnosis is by communicating with the subconscious mind effectively, which can be done using pre-recorded hypnosis weight loss programs or self-hypnosis. An established program will repeat suggestions to your subconscious that can be layered while you are already in a hypnotic state. If you practice self-hypnosis, you will need to create your own suggestions geared specifically for your situation.

When creating your own suggestions, word choice is important. When you formulate a suggestion you will utilize specific words because of how they are acted upon in the subconscious.

Four of the most important words you can use are:

• Imagine

• Because

• Don't

• Now

Here's why –

Imagine is used to get past the subconscious's anti-suggestive wall and right to whatever follows in the sentence. Imagine isn't viewed as a command to the subconscious and is interpreted more as "you don't have to do what I'm saying, simply consider it." But in reality, what it does is it opens the door to the subconscious which allows the remainder of the sentence to flow through easily. This means that the suggestions you make using the word imagine are more likely to be received and acted upon by the subconscious.

An imagine example for weight loss is:

"Imagine that when I experience sadness I now take a stroll around the block in place of putting food in my mouth."

Because is used to satisfy the mind's desire for a cause-and-effect relationship in logic. This is used strategically to create a suggestion that the subconscious will act upon. A because example for weight loss is:

"I will consume less because I can see myself a dress size smaller in the next few weeks."

Don't is used when creating suggestions because it is considered a command. The reasoning behind using don't is similar to that with a child. If you tell the subconscious not to feel a certain way, there is frequently resistance with a "don't tell me how to feel" response, and the action to do the opposite. Pop culture calls this don't technique "reverse psychology."

A don't example for weight loss is:

"Don't feel required to exercise everyday."

Now is used to create change in the behavior that is linked to the subconscious.

A now example for weight loss is:

"Now when I get behind the wheel of the car I will feel compelled to drink water."

Treatment of Insomnia

Lack of sleep and insomnia are an escalating problem in our modern world. As with stress reduction techniques, a state of hypnosis can help regular people quiet the cacophony of their inner minds, and finally allow themselves to get some restful sleep. But don't worry – you will always wake up when you need to!

One easy way to get to sleep that is extremely popular with people everywhere is progressive relaxation. This method is used by many people that don't even realize that this relaxation technique is used in the induction and deepening of hypnosis.

Start by completely relaxing your body in bed. Close your eyes. Slowly start at the top of your head and work your way to your toes, recognizing and putting each body part to sleep. Concentrate on breathing and regulating breath. Most people end this practice feeling calm and relaxed, with a mind that is no longer racing but instead blank and ready for sleep to take over.

Stress Reduction

Hypnosis by its very nature is a deep state of relaxation, and hence a very powerful tool for stress reduction. Without much effort, or needing to go very deep into a trance, you can experience a very relaxed state of mind. With practice, you can call on these stress reduction techniques at will.

Recently, stress related problems at work have been identified as a crippling problem in the corporate environment. Lost work days due to stress-related illnesses, overtired employees that are underproductive, and burnt-out workers constitute a workforce that is on edge.

How can you use hypnosis to improve your response to stressful situations? Hypnosis can be used as an educational tool that will teach you what to do when you get stressed out. Hypnosis will also add to your belief system the options you have for handling each stressful situation in your life.

There are essentially three choices when in a stressful situation. You can either deal with it in the moment, wait until a more appropriate time or location presents itself to deal with the stress, or let the situation go and forgive and forget.

Stress is instantly reduced when hypnosis is induced. Both mental and physical evidence indicates that the simple act of being hypnotized greatly reduces overall stress on the body.

Improvement of Memory and Learning

We all have trouble recalling information from time to time.

The information you are trying to retrieve is usually not forgotten. Once the bit of information is recalled, we realize we knew it all along. By using hypnotic techniques people can teach themselves to have instant recall of any fact, and better filing of that information in their own minds in the future.

There are hypnotic tools that can be used to increase your effectiveness in learning, memory, and recall. All of us are capable of learning at our own pace and capacity.

Undoubtedly, most people could stand to improve their learning abilities.

Using the senses together is an excellent way to improve learning capabilities. It is said that people remember less than 25% of what they read. Did you also know that:

• People remember as much as 65% of what they do themselves.

• People remember 50% of what they say.

• People remember 45% of what they see.

• People remember 33% of what they hear.

It is also known that if a person uses all of their senses in conjunction with one another, they will remember up to 90%. This means that when you are learning something new you should try to make it appeal to all of your senses.

Use these tools to help you learn better. When reading, engage in self-dialogue periodically. Close your eyes and visualize what is being said in the book. Visualize yourself doing what you are reading about. Create self-talk that involves you providing commentary on what you are learning. Even try to picture yourself teaching to someone else what you are learning. It is widely known that the best way to really learn something is to teach it.

Hypnosis can also be used to adjust your attitude about learning. Do you always take a negative stance when thinking about going to school, or learning something new on the job? This is probably the number one barrier that is making it harder for you to learn. By changing the established set of beliefs that you have in place in your subconscious, you can reprogram yourself to feel confident learning.

The best plan of action of incorporating hypnosis into your learning experiences is to use hypnosis prior to beginning a large learning endeavor. If you know you are about to begin a training session or learning experience, practice hypnosis using suggestions that focus on a new, positive attitude about learning.

Workplace Performance

In corporate America today, hypnosis has many potential applications that can help increase productivity, improve job performance, and enhance employee job satisfaction.

These positive changes mean:

• Less turnover of qualified workers, because they are happier with their jobs.

• More productive employees that get more done with less hours. This is perfect in times of hiring freezes and lay-offs.

• Better job performance that creates a smooth, well-oiled business function. If everyone is working to their full potential, free of emotional baggage that seeps into the workplace, then all employees can focus on the task at hand.

Hypnosis can be used in the workplace to help an employee become a better decision maker. Decisions vary by importance, and both small and large decision-making ability can be helped by hypnosis.

We live our lives in patterns that dictate the rhythm of our day. Throughout the course of the day, we are presented with decisions. The decisions can be as simple as "Iced or hot coffee?" or as complicated as "Should I transfer to Tokyo?"

Some people thrive in the ability to make a decision on the spot and stand by it, making it work and flourishing in the process. Others need to analyze and reanalyze the pros and cons of the decision, spending months thinking, only to make a choice and doubt the validity of the decision.

No matter where you fall in the spectrum between these two examples, your subconscious mind plays a major role in your decision-making process.

To become a better decision maker through hypnosis, use these steps:

Step 1:

Identify and organize your ideal value system.

For a consistency to your decision making ability, you will need to make decisions with a sturdy value system in place. Everyone has a value system, and even if you can't explain yours or think you may not have one, you do.

If you cross-reference your value system to your decision, you will ask yourself (either consciously or subconsciously) the following questions:

1. Who is important to you?

2. What is significant to you?

3. What is the order of importance of the things and people in your life?

Put your personal values in order from most to least important. Next, we will compare them with our actual values as demonstrated through our actions.

Step 2:

Compare your perceived values to your actual values.

Actual values are those where you pay the greatest amount of attention, spend the most time, or exude the most energy. Oftentimes, these are not what we want to be our priority, but are.

This often happens with children and work. A working mom will say the most important thing is her life is her children, however, if she rarely spends time with them, she is actually making whatever else she is spending time on more important. It's a difficult situation that occurs often and results in a dual value system, overall life dissatisfaction, and stress.

When comparing the two lists, ask yourself where the major discrepancies are and why. After doing this comparison, how will you change how you make decisions about yourself and your time?

When making decisions, you will probably be faced with decisions where what you want is not what you feel to be the right thing to do. This conflict and gap between what's right and what you want to do should ultimately become smaller after working through it with hypnosis.

Another component that you should understand about what goes into the decision-making process is the connection between decisions and emotions.

You have probably heard that you should make decisions with your head and not your heart. While you should make an effort to balance and include some emotion in your decision-making process, the ultimate decision should be determined by the rational side rather than the emotional one.

When your lists of ideal and actual values are similar and nearly the same, your emotions can give you valuable feedback in the decision-making process. You can also then make decisions more easily. When faced with a decision, simply ask – "How does this impact what is important to me? Does it add to my priorities or take away from them?"

Here are some tools to include in your thought process when making a decision:

• Make sure your values match your overall goals.

• Decide if the decision really needs to be made urgently. Take your time and think for a moment. Is this perceived urgency? Does a decision really even need to be made at all?

• If you feel pressured, determine the root of the pressure and deal with it.

• Use hypnosis to also help you build confidence in your decision-making process.

Another major issue in the workplace is procrastination.

Putting off what should be done creates hours upon hours of underproductive time in the office. At home, procrastination prevents us from getting ahead personally. No matter where you find you are procrastinating, hypnosis can help you put an end to it.

How do you break the cycle of procrastination, and stop it from wrecking your life? Try these tips:

1. Pinpoint what behavior you want to change in yourself.

2. Identify and visualize what you will do instead.

3. Don't fear success!

4. Use self-hypnosis to create positive self-talk.

5. Suggest a "do it now" attitude.

Hypnosis in the workplace can also be used to help an employee avoid procrastination and "do it now!"

Hypnosis and Pain Control

Pain is how the body tells the mind that we need to pay closer attention to ourselves. Hypnosis can be used to reduce or eliminate the pain you experience in daily life, or when doing activities you enjoy.

Often times I will hear people say hypnosis isn't any different than the placebo effect. A number of research projects have proven that incorrect.

In 1969, Thomas H. McGlashan and his colleagues at the University of Pennsylvania found that for those individuals on the lower levels of hypnotizability, hypnosis was as potent in reducing pain as a sugar pill they had been instructed was a powerful painkiller. In addition, highly hypnotizable volunteers received three times the benefit from hypnosis as from the placebo.

In 1996, The National Institute of Health Technology assessment panel judged hypnosis to be a valuable tool for alleviating pain from cancer and other chronic conditions.

Extensive clinical studies also testify that hypnosis can reduce the pain experienced by burn patients as well as children with bone marrow issues, and to assist women in labor to reduce, or even remove, pain.

In the International Journal of Clinical and Experimental Hypnosis, a study revealed that hypnotic suggestions relieved 75 percent of the pain for 933 subjects in a total of 27 different experiments. The pain relief effects of hypnotic suggestion are valuable and important. In some cases the degree of relief exceeded that provided by morphine.

What makes hypnosis successful in relation to experiencing pain? Any reduction in pain is considered a success. Relief from pain is not always immediate, so if you do not experience immediate results, continue trying different types of hypnosis. On the other hand, many people experience immediate relief from all sorts of pain, and swear by hypnosis as their pain reliever of choice.

Research has determined that hypnosis can be an exceptional pain reliever.

Childbirth

I would not let any of my loved ones go into childbirth without the use of hypnosis; it is simply too easy to apply these techniques to help create a satisfying experience for the expectant mother. For instance, with hypnosis you can program nine months of comfortable expectation, eliminate the fear of the birthing process, reduce the discomfort of contractions, and help to create the ultimate bonding experience between mother and baby.

How exactly do you use hypnosis during pregnancy and labor? First and foremost, understand that hypnosis complements modern day medicine – it doesn't replace it.

Use these techniques in conjunction with your doctor or midwife to create the best possible situation.

During pregnancy, use hypnosis in the following ways:

1. Use visualization techniques, and suggestions with the subconscious to relieve yourself of morning sickness.

Suggest the relief of pregnancy symptoms.

2. Reduce back aches and sciatica pain and discomfort through relaxation and suggestion.

3. High blood pressure, tension and stress often go hand-in-hand during pregnancy. Use hypnosis to reduce blood pressure through meditation, relaxation, and visualization.

4. Insomnia is a common problem associated with late pregnancy. Use the calming effects of hypnosis to refocus the mind during sleep time. Practice progressive relaxation to steer the mind toward sleep.

5. It has even been said that breech pregnancies can be turned without needing a version procedure.

Visualizing the fetus moving "head down" can help encourage the turning movement.

Every woman's birthing experience is different. Pregnancies and births even vary from one child to another for the same woman.

The main way that hypnosis can work for all women in any stage of pregnancy or labor is through relaxation. These hypnosis techniques establish a tool for coping with pain and discomfort so that when the expectant mother experiences pain or discomfort she can remove and reduce it by deep relaxation through hypnosis.

Here are some points to remember:

• Realize that you can never gain control over labor, it is a function of the body that is instinctual and physical and cannot be controlled.

• Replace the desire to control your body during birth with the concept of release. The real purpose of labor is to release the baby from the body. Focus your relaxation effort during the release.

• Relaxing during the release allows you to save energy for the last stage of delivery. It also helps your muscles relax. If you are not fighting for control, you body can more easily do its job.

• Practice getting into a relaxed state and self-hypnosis in advance of delivery so that you can easily slip into this state during labor.

When getting started, practice these methods of hypnosis:

Step 1:

Practice progressive relaxation.

For the duration of your pregnancy, try to practice this relaxation technique for a smooth, stress-reduced pregnancy. Once you go into labor, you will be well-versed in calming your mind so that your body can do its work unhindered.

In a calm space with low lights and soft music, find a comfortable position. Focus on your breathing. Work from your head down, slowly relaxing and calming each and every body part. This common induction technique for hypnosis is highly effective in providing an all-over calmness to your body.

Step 2:

Create a self-hypnosis "trigger" word.

Often hypnosis entertainment shows demonstrate the use of a trigger word that is used by the hypnotists to quickly induce hypnosis without having a long induction process.

You can take advantage of this same practice by creating your own trigger word. It doesn't even need to be a word – it can be an action or a picture. Some people will take a cleansing breath and count back from four for a quicker induction. Keep it simple, and try to do it the same way every time.

Step 3:

Deal with the fear of childbirth.

Many first-time moms are afraid of what will happen during labor. They get nervous about the childbirth process itself, the mom's own safety, the baby's well-being during birthing, the pain – everything!

Getting a handle on the anxiety associated with childbirth is a goal of hypnosis. Fear causes tension in the body, and as previously discussed, tension and stress hinders the body's natural process of labor.

The first thing you can do to relieve some of the fear surrounding childbirth is to remove the unknown. Educate yourself through reading, classes, videos, and other sources about the physical process of labor. This way you can respond to the physical cues as your body gives them.

Make an effort to deal with your negative attitudes toward childbirth in the subconscious through hypnosis well before delivery. This will help you keep a calm mind and body.

Focus on visualization and imagine yourself in a safe and comfortable place. Create your own birthing experience without the background horror stories of someone else's negative opinion.

Step 4:

Deepen your hypnotic state using images.

Use a variety of deepening techniques to create a deeper state of hypnosis to help you through the labor and birth.

Try visualizing one of these images:

Running water

Water always has a calming connotation. Envision waterfalls, streams, and ocean waves. Hear the sounds and feel the movement. Contractions are often described as waves that come over the body – use this in your imagery to anticipate and allow each to wash over you.

Blooming flowers

The slowed down process of a flower blooming can help your mind and body move through the process of the baby moving through the birthing canal.

Use hypnosis during childbirth to change the way the brain perceives the messages being sent from the body.

Smoking Cessation

Hands down, the number one question I'm asked after spectators have witnessed amazing hypnosis demonstrations at my performances is whether hypnosis can help them quit smoking.

I'm happy to report that I have indeed helped people across the country with a very effective hypnosis-based solution.

At the heart of it are the ritual habits smokers have with their smoking. The physical addiction can be gutted through with sheer willpower in a matter of days. However, many smokers relapse weeks or months later, when they can't resist the temptation of having a cigarette while participating in an activity during which they'd usually smoked in the past.

By using hypnosis to break free of these associations and see themselves as the non-smoker they now are, they will simply not even entertain that idea any longer.

Fears & Phobias

If there is a genuine reason and rationale for someone being afraid, it is considered a fear. However, if there is no rational reason behind an extreme fear, it is called a phobia.

Many people today live with debilitating phobias. Some common phobias include:

• Agoraphobia – the fear of places where escape might be difficult or unavailable in case of emergency.

• Claustrophobia – the fear of being contained in a small space.

• Arachnophobia – an extreme fear of spiders.

• Necrophobia – an extreme fear of the dead.

Hypnosis is highly effective in rewriting the underlying beliefs behind fears and phobias. After several sessions focusing on removing a phobia or fear, a subject will notice a substantial improvement in their daily life. Fears and phobias often disappear when hypnosis is effectively used.

Self-Confidence & Self-Esteem

Self-confidence is defined as the belief that you can accomplish something. Self-esteem is the belief that you are deserving and worthy to be alive.

How can hypnosis impact your levels of self-esteem and self-confidence? By working on your own beliefs about yourself, you can change the negative thoughts and reprogram your mind to think positive things.

Self-confidence is essential for everyone – especially working people who need on-the-job confidence to perform well at work. One highly effective way to create such confidence is through modeling. Here's how to do it.

Step 1:

Think of a colleague, friend, or someone else you emulate for their unshakeable self-confidence.

Close your eyes and think about the person you admire for their confidence level.

Step 2:

Replay how your mentor acts when demonstrating self-confidence.

Picture the way they move their arms, talk, and use their eyes. What do they do with their hands?

What types of words do they use that exude self-confidence?

How do they communicate with others?

Step 3:

In a self-hypnotic state, visualize stepping inside of them.

Picture yourself taking on the traits of self-confidence that you admire in your colleague, friend, or mentor.

Step 4:

Practice this newly found confidence level throughout one day.

Pay special attention to those you interact with. You will probably notice a newly found respect from others. A more confident you will probably make others around you feel more comfortable when interacting with you.

Prosperity Awareness

Having enough of the resources you need to live to the standard in which you desire is the key to living life prosperously. Prosperity is not about monetary wealth; although having enough money to lead the life you want is the main theory behind being prosperous.

Life prosperity includes the following:

• Feeling comfortable and happy with life.

• An overall less complicated existence because the family finances are in order. There are no large debts like looming credit cards to fear.

• High levels of health and well-being.

• A happy home environment.

Hypnosis can help you have a better understanding of money and its relationship to you and happiness. Money is a belief of value. If everyone believes that the dollar bill has a certain value, then it does. Of course it is backed by gold – which we also believe has value. It's true because the world believes it to be true.

There are financial ways that you can set yourself up to be financially established. In order to have more money, consider the following:

1. Reduce unnecessary expenses.

2. Analyze your household budget, and make necessary changes.

3. Invest in areas that are secure, yet have some risk.

These typically offer the highest yield. Mutual funds, real estate, etc.

4. Try to stop or reduce high interest rates.

5. Save for tomorrow, today. Always pay yourself out of each paycheck.

The most important point about being aware of your prosperity is that money will not make you happy. In fact, a large percentage of lottery winners say that money actually made their lives less fulfilling and satisfying. Don't look at life success with dollar signs. Count a prosperous life as one that is happy and rich in personal relationships and comfort.

So how does hypnosis tie into the awareness of your prosperity, you ask? The best way to become financially and emotionally prosperous is to first know the basics about money and make wise choices, and secondly to focus within, through hypnosis, about your attitudes surrounding money and success. When creating a life for long-term pleasure, the behaviors you exhibit regarding finances are positively impacted by hypnosis.

Use hypnosis to visualize your prosperous life. During your hypnotic trace, you will be given suggestions about the "right" amount of money that you need to enable you to have security and the lifestyle that you genuinely want to live.

Hypnosis is also used to address your negative attitudes about people with money.

Use hypnosis to motivate yourself to get your financial house in order, no matter how disordered it is. Some people simply need a little nudge to reorganize themselves, and others need to pull themselves up from the ashes. Whatever the case may be, use hypnosis to help you get on the right track.

Psychotherapy & Hypnosis

Hypnosis can also boost the effectiveness of psychotherapy for some conditions. Traditional medicine often works in conjunction with hypnosis via a written doctor's referral and a two-pronged approach to the patient's problem – both physical and mental. There are also plenty of non-medical benefits from hypnosis.

Exciting work is now being done to incorporate hypnotic trances into mental healing. Psychotherapeutic interchange is one way that hypnosis is being used effectively. Hypnosis is used in the beginning investigative stage, the midway stage of working through the issue at hand, and the final termination phase. In psychotherapy, hypnosis is used in addition to non-hypnotic work such as counseling and medical evaluation.

The therapist's first goal in working with a subject is to identify what the core issues are. Hypnosis is an excellent tool that is often used to get at the root of the problem.

Remember, the symptom that the subject is trying to fix is usually just the behavior of a greater belief or value held within.

Eighteen different studies found that patients who received hypnosis in addition to their cognitive behavioral therapy for disorders such as insomnia, obesity, and anxiety, showed higher improvement than 70 percent of the patients who utilized psychotherapy alone.

You may be familiar with other uses of hypnosis such as overcoming the fear of dentistry or creating a proper sales mindset. You may have even heard about using hypnosis to improve a golf game. Whatever your reason for utilizing hypnosis, you will find it can make a major impact on the quality of your life.

To keep yourself safe, you should never self-medicate and should always seek your doctor's advice before beginning any type of treatment.

Hypnosis as Entertainment

Beyond its medical and clinical applications, hypnosis has a long and distinguished history as a unique form of audience participation entertainment. There's no other way known to literally take strangers from an audience and with no prior arrangements and make them the stars of the show.

Hypnotists have been entertaining at fairs and other public venues for well over a century. More recently they have become very popular at more conservative venues such as corporate events, meetings, conventions, or school functions.

Trusted hypnotic entertainers will never make fun of a volunteer or make a joke at their expense, nor will they perform dangerous stunts.

What they will do is offer an incredible way to boost morale and break the ice with a well-planned program. They will help create camaraderie amongst work and social groups, and break down the interpersonal walls by removing the hierarchy on the group and treating everyone as equals.

Hypnosis show participants don't have to worry about being forced to do things outside of their principles. No hypnotist can take a person's fundamental subconscious values and make that person do something against their will. If there is a major subconscious resistance, the hypnotized subject will not follow a subconscious command by the hypnotist.

Entertainment hypnosis is a fun way to see already extroverted people do or say things in front of an audience that they would probably not normally do, and help draw introverted people out of their shyness. Since people typically volunteer for such an activity, or they at least agree to go up on stage in front of others to be hypnotized, they are clearly willing to participate, which makes them a good candidate for hypnosis.

It is important to remember that a participant of stage hypnosis will not do anything that is against his or her fundamental morals and principles in the subconscious mind.

When looking to hire a hypnotic entertainer for your own events, be sure to ask for their testimonials. Ensure that you're getting a tested and proven program performed by a modern, faster-paced entertainer who respects their volunteers and audience. Then get ready for the time of your life!

5

Hypnosis and You

You may be thinking, "Hypnosis sounds wonderful, but can I be hypnotized? I don't think I can be. I'm very stubborn, I don't have a good attention span and I hate to give up control." Remind yourself that you already experience hypnosis on a daily basis.

Hypnosis is not witchcraft, manipulation or magic. It simply is a tool that will allow you to tap into the power of your mind.

What Is Required to Be Hypnotized?

All that is required to be hypnotized is willingness and a minimum IQ level of 60.

If you don't have the willingness, then you will not concentrate on reaching this state of mind. Consequently, you won't. Nobody can be hypnotized against their will.

If you happen to be the sort of person who does not have a high level of hypnotizability, then being hypnotized is still within reach; it merely means a longer time period may be required to access that special state of mind. You can enter the trance state whenever you desire. Sounds, lights and external disturbances can themselves be incorporated into the hypnotic process called an induction.

Oftentimes incorporating these distractions will make the hypnotic state easier to reach and more satisfying.

How Does It Feel To Be Hypnotized?

I'm sure you have seen zombie-like characters in the movies and on television that are supposedly in a hypnotic trance.

This common misconception can create resistance in those who are being hypnotized for the first time.

It can be hard to allow yourself to relax if you think that under hypnosis you will surrender all control of your behavior to the hypnotist.

In fact, when you are hypnotized, you are in more control than when you are in your normal daily state. You become internally focused and your surrounding environment becomes insignificant.

If for any reason there was an emergency or your attention was needed, you would immediately emerge yourself to respond appropriately. (Emerge means to come to a full waking state.) People in a hypnotized state may appear to be asleep, but the biological state of sleep is very different from hypnosis.

While your body is relaxed, your mind will be fully alert and aware of the suggestions it is receiving. All outside stimulus will become irrelevant. Your focus will be directly on the words of the suggestions you are receiving and your breathing will be light and rhythmic.

You may have a distorted sense of time. You may feel like you have been in hypnosis for just a couple minutes, even if it has been sixty to ninety minutes.

Now that you know what it feels like, it's time to learn how to hypnotize yourself.

Pre-Hypnosis Planning

Before practicing hypnosis, you will need to ask yourself some questions to get the most out of your session:

1. Are you going to go to a hypnotist, hypnotherapist, or practice self-hypnosis?

Make your choice based on what is most accessible and what you are most comfortable with.

2. Where will you practice hypnosis?

Find a quiet spot where you can be free of external sounds and stimulus for at least one hour.

3. What are the goals of the session?

Pick one thing that you want to work on, identify it, and focus on it.

4. What will you use for content during your session?

If you go to a hypnotist, they will guide you through hypnosis. If you decide to try self-hypnosis, you can either use a recorded audio soundtrack with induction, suggestion, and awakening language or you can prerecord your own.

How to Hypnotize Yourself

It is now time for you to experience self-hypnosis.

Following the self-hypnosis instruction below, I will coach you on where, when, and how to apply this technique for maximum effectiveness.

It is easiest to break down the self-hypnosis process into five components:

1. Mindset

2. Induction

3. Deepening

4. Suggestions

5. Awakening

Mindset

You must be willing to be hypnotized. Your mindset should support your hypnosis session by focusing on the goal you wish to achieve, regardless of whether that is a specific change in your behavior (goal-oriented such as weight loss) or just simple relaxation. Consider the goal of your session, the outcome you desire, and be expectation of reaching your goal.

If you doubt you will succeed or if you second-guess yourself you will find yourself in that situation. Approach this exercise correctly and you will succeed.

It is just like everything in life. Our mindset can help us soar or hold us back. Luckily that is in our control.

Make a commitment right now to succeed and I have no doubt that you will. Perhaps you will even surprise yourself by how easy a hypnotic state is to achieve and how quickly you are able to do it.

Are you ready? If not, take a few more minutes until you are. Only then is it the right time to continue. When you are ready, let's get started; you are going to really enjoy this!

Induction

The induction is what you will use to turn your focus from external to internal. The induction will allow you to tap into the power of your mind to reach your desired outcome by programming your subconscious. And we know what is programmed on a subconscious level will automatically be adopted by your conscious mind.

Here is an overview of your self-hypnosis induction:

Close your eyes and slowly relax every muscle in your entire body. Consciously direct yourself to relax every muscle from your toes, feet, calves, over your knees, up your thighs, your mid-section, your lower back, your upper back, your shoulders, down your biceps, over your wrists, all the way to the tips of your fingers, up through your neck, over your jaw, through every muscle in your face and around your eyes.

Allow every muscle to relax from the top of your head down to the tips of your toes.

Just allow yourself to systematically relax and enjoy it.

Don't be in a hurry to complete this process. Depending on your time constraints it should take from two to eight minutes.

Tell yourself, *"The more I relax, the deeper I go, the deeper I go, the better I feel. I'm growing more and more relaxed with every easy breath I exhale."*

Don't force it to happen; the more you let go, the easier it is.

Just allow yourself to completely release all tension.

I will then have you think of a time when you were relaxed.

Maybe it was on a vacation or day off.

You should use each of your senses to relive that experience.

For example, perhaps you were relaxing on a hike, surrounded by vibrant green trees and a gentle bubbling brook. You should imagine you hear the sounds of the running stream and the wildlife in your mind.

Relive that experience, feel the slight breeze as it rolls over you, feel the ground beneath you and smell the fresh outdoors.

Or perhaps you recall a time when you were indoors, resting peacefully, taking a bath and just relaxing.

Perhaps you feel the warmth of water, maybe you smell the fragrance of the bubble bath, hear the sound of the gentle music in the background while you are letting your mind float a million miles away....

As you remember these pleasant experiences, you will find yourself changing on a physiological level and becoming very relaxed and focused.

Final suggestions in this phase to give yourself are:

"The deeper you go, the more satisfying it becomes. You feel comfortable and relaxed.

You continue to release all tension with every thought you have.

Allowing yourself to drop down deeper and deeper with every easy breath you take and every sound you hear.

If you need to awaken, you can do that simply by counting yourself up from one to five, and you will awaken feeling refreshed and energized."

You should repeat these final suggestions from one to three times and then move onto deepening your trance state.

Deepening Your Hypnotic State

In order to deepen your hypnotic trance state you should provide yourself with the following suggestion:

"With each count from five to one, you will drop down twice as deep."

Imagine yourself stepping down a staircase and say to yourself,

"As I descend this staircase, I will drop down deeper; with each step I take down I descend to a place of peace and contentment."

"Five - letting go of everything"

"Four - feeling light, distant, relaxed"

"Three - dropping down deeper than ever before"

"Two - from here out, with every step down I will drop twice as deep as before."

"One - all the way down, more relaxed than ever, feeling peaceful and content."

I would recommend that you repeat this deepening process three times. You will start to feel detached. Anyone watching you will notice that your breathing pattern has become light. Your heart rate has become altered and your blood pressure has reduced. You are in a state of hypnosis.

I would recommend that with every self-hypnosis session you do, you always give yourself the suggestion:

"I will drop down deeper and deeper with each session, faster and faster."

With repeated hypnosis sessions, you will find yourself dropping down into wonderful and peaceful states of hypnotic trance quickly.

Initially, you may wonder if you are really hypnotized. This is completely natural. If you are following the instructions on the previous pages, you can rest assured you are hypnotized. In addition, in the coming pages I will teach you how to prove to yourself you are in a hypnotic trance.

Many people wonder how deep they have to be in order to receive the benefits of hypnotic suggestions. Studies show even in light trance depth you will receive the wonderful benefits of hypnosis.

To make this process easy for you I will provide you with a full self-hypnosis induction script. You will be able to read it verbatim. You can choose to learn it or you can choose to record it and listen to it during your self-hypnosis session.

Either way works fine. And then, once you are hypnotized, it is important that we take advantage of the hypnotized state so you get the maximum value from hypnosis. You do that with suggestions.

Hypnotic Suggestions

Prior to your hypnotic trance you want to form your hypnotic suggestions. Your suggestions should always be phrased in the positive, never in the negative. You should also phrase them in the present, never in the past or future.

The following is an incorrect and correct example of a weight loss suggestion for your comparison.

Incorrect Example:

"I'm on my way to losing weight and giving up foods that are bad for me."

Correct Example:

"I weigh 180 pounds and find greater satisfaction with smaller portions."

In the incorrect example, you will notice it is phrased in the negative, referring to giving up foods and losing weight. In addition, you will notice the incorrect phrase of timing.

Your subconscious mind will hear these suggestions and take them literally. It will think you are on your way, but it's not time yet to lose the weight.

The following is a suggestion that can be used for controlling stress. Compare the correct and incorrect examples.

Incorrect Example:

"My life will be less stressed when I worry less about those professional and personal worries that are out of my control."

Correct Example:

"I control my stress level and release those things I cannot control."

Think about which areas of your life you would like to improve and then work on one specific area during your trance session. Don't work on multiple tasks in the same trance session.

Some people think, "I'll work on stress, pain control and weight loss during the same session." It is too much and you will dilute the value.

Think of the specific goal you would like to achieve. Record that goal. Then start to structure suggestions that will allow you to achieve it. Be positive, be present, and be brief.

Edit your suggestions down to simple sentences. In a typical trance session you should use no more than four suggestions that support the single goal you have chosen.

Repetition of each suggestion is important to achieve that desired goal. Repeat each suggestion six to eight times per self-hypnosis session.

Awakening

The final step in self-hypnosis is to awaken yourself. You do that by giving yourself the following suggestion:

"In a moment I will count from one to five. I will awaken feeling refreshed, energized and looking forward to my next session. I am allowing myself now to fully integrate each suggestion I have provided which supports my goal."

"With every session I will find myself dropping down deeper, faster and enjoying it more and more."

"One, imagining that I'm back at home just like I am every morning; two, allowing the energy to fill my limbs; three, becoming more aware of my surroundings; four, appreciating the time I spend for myself and the value it provides; five, wide awake and noticing how good I feel."

Congratulations on your trance session. In five steps you have programmed your mind to help you accomplish your goals. Don't underestimate the power of this formula; research has proven its effectiveness!

How Can I Prove To Myself That I'm Really Hypnotized?

Here is an advanced, little-known technique that you can use to confirm you are in a state of hypnosis.

This test should occur after the deepening component and prior to the behavior change suggestions.

Give yourself the suggestion that as you relax, your mouth will begin to fill with saliva and as you swallow it will take you down deeper.

If your mouth begins to fill with saliva then you know you are hypnotized and responding to suggestion!

How Long Should My Trance State Last?

There is no set time requirement for a hypnotic session. It only takes a couple of minutes to enter this state of mind and program yourself for success.

Be sure to allow enough time for you to reach a hypnotic state and do the work that you want to do. You don't want to feel rushed, and if you have a time limit, you will not reach a complete stage of relaxation because you are thinking about the clock.

You will develop your own pattern for self-hypnosis as you become experienced with it. When I'm at home and on my regular schedule, I prefer to do twenty minute hypnotic sessions. If my schedule will not permit this length of time, then I experience a quick five or ten minute session.

Where Should I Experience Trance?

It's important to think about where you will experience a hypnotic trance in advance of experiencing it. For obvious reasons, never experience hypnosis while driving or operating any machinery.

Many people use hypnosis during their normal daytime activities such as when they are on a break at work, or on a bus, or airplane. Others reserve it as a special time in their day where they can completely relax and recharge.

If you will be using hypnosis at home, I recommend you experience your trance session seated or reclined in a chair, couch, or bed. Let your significant other or kids know you are not to be disturbed unless an emergency occurs. This is your time for yourself, so enjoy it.

How Many Sessions are Recommended for Permanent Results?

Every individual is different, and there is no right or wrong answer to this question. As a guideline, I recommend you work on one specific change (weight loss, confidence, etc.) for twenty-one days straight. Research shows this is the opportune length of time to achieve your goal and cause permanent behavioral change.

If after this amount of time you find you need to continue with hypnosis in order to continue to achieve positive results, stick with it. You are the only one who knows for certain when you have made a successful permanent change.

Obviously, before making any changes in your medical or physical well-being, you should consult your physician.

6

Hypnotizing Others

Hypnotizing Others

With some of the following scripts, you can not only hypnotize yourself but also hypnotize others.

When hypnotizing someone else, be sure to first determine the behavior they are trying to change, and then look to what might be the root of the problem. Use this information when choosing which suggestions to use.

If you choose to use a pre-written script like those that are provided within this chapter, simply make yourself or your subject comfortable and get started.

If you are hypnotizing someone else, be sure they understand what to expect from the experience. Explain what they will and will not get out of hypnosis. If they have never been hypnotized in the past, explain the process and how hypnosis works. Better yet, encourage the subject to read this book!

How to Tell When People are Hypnotized

Once you begin the induction process, how will you know that the person you are hypnotizing is hypnotized? Many people ask, "How do you know if people are really hypnotized? Can't they just fake it?"

Yes, they could try to fake it, but it is very easy to see for the trained hypnotist. It's more than we can go into within this book, but here is one study that you will find interesting.

Taru Kinnunen, Harold S. Zamansky and their colleagues at Northeastern University conducted a study on "faking" hypnosis. They utilized a lie detector to measure the response of hypnotized and faking (unhypnotized) subjects.

While faking hypnosis, the lie detector revealed the subject's responses as it traditionally would. However, when used on the hypnotized subjects the lie detector could not detect the truth from the lies.

This proved that when a hypnotized person is provided with suggestions, their full psychological system reacts appropriately and supports the truth of those suggestions.

There doesn't appear to be a difference internally to real events or fantasy events created by hypnotic subjects.

Hypnosis Induction Scripts

In the following pages I have given you an actual hypnosis induction script. You can use it to hypnotize yourself or to hypnotize others. You may learn it and recite it on your own, read it aloud, or record the script and play it back during your hypnosis session.

Now that you know the components of self-hypnosis, you will recognize them as they are used in this script. You should insert your own suggestions to work on what you desire. You will be prompted on the customizable suggestion.

The following script is referred to as a progressive relaxation script. It is a script commonly used by many hypnotist to slowly relax a person into hypnosis.

In Appendix B, I present another type of script, called the "modified Dave Elman" induction. The Dave Elman script was created many years ago but is still used by many professional hypnotherapists today.

Hypnotic Induction Script

Take a nice deep breath, and as you exhale, allow your eyes to close. Listen to the sound of my voice. Just allow yourself to relax more and more with every easy breath you exhale, and every word I say, appreciating how good it feels, just to allow yourself to relax. Appreciating the time you spend for yourself, appreciating the way you feel, and allowing yourself to become more and more relaxed with every easy breath you exhale, and every word I say. I want you to notice how you needn't do anything, you can just let go. Direct your attention toward your left foot. Notice how that left foot feels. I want you to relax that left foot completely, allowing every muscle throughout your entire left foot to just relax, relaxing all muscles and all joints throughout your entire left foot, noticing how good that feels.

I want you to push that relaxation up over your ankle and into your left calf. Perhaps you start to notice how that left foot perhaps feels heavy, and perhaps you start to notice how that left foot may feel heavy or light, or may not even seem to exist, and that takes you down deeper, and the deeper you go, the more comfortable, the more secure you feel, and the deeper you go, the more comfortable and secure you feel, just allowing that left foot, that left calf muscle to completely relax.

Now, pushing that relaxation over your knee and into your left thigh, feeling so good in every way. I want you to direct your attention toward your right foot. Relax that right foot totally, relaxing all the joints, relaxing all the muscles throughout your entire right foot. I want you to push that relaxation up over your right calf, and I want you to push that relaxation over your right ankle, and right over your right calf, every muscle loose, every joint relaxed. The more relaxed you become, the deeper you go. The deeper you go, the more confident, the more secure you feel.

I want you to push that relaxation now up into your right thigh, pushing that relaxation, just noticing how your legs are starting to settle in, how they needn't do anything but relax, and perhaps, you begin to notice your left foot, and as you do, it takes you down to a more pleasant state of mind.

Perhaps you become aware of your right foot.

Your entire lower body feeling so serene, so peaceful, pushing that relaxation up into your pelvis area, right up into your abdomen area, relaxing all your stomach muscles now, just allowing all muscles to go loose, limp, relax, noticing how good it feels, directing some attention straight up over the entire middle of your torso, allowing your shoulders to completely relax, directing particular attention towards your left shoulder, allowing those muscles and that joint to completely go loose, limp. Relax.

Allowing those fingers throughout your left hand to be completely free of any strain, allowing your left hand completely and totally to relax, and allowing that relaxation to wash up over your wrist, and into your forearm, and across your bicep, and across your bicep, allowing that left arm to be completely loose, limp, relaxed. Directing special attention now towards your right shoulder, just allowing all stress to be released, and allowing that right shoulder to go completely limp, allowing all muscles throughout your entire right hand to just let go.

Allowing the joints to just be completely relaxed, and pushing that relaxation up over your wrist, and across your forearm, and over your bicep, completely relaxing, relaxing, feeling wonderful, and allowing all strain from your lower back, now to just disappear.

Allowing the entire back area to relax, allowing your shoulder blade, allowing your entire back area to just relax, allowing every muscle throughout your neck, allowing every muscle throughout your neck to just let go. And, pushing that relaxation up into your face now, allowing your cheeks to relax, allowing all those small little muscles around your eye to just go limp, allowing those muscles around your eyes to just go limp, relaxing them, noticing how good that feels, relaxing your forehead, relaxing your cheek muscles, relaxing your jaw.

And now, sending a pleasant wave of relaxation from the top of your head, all the way down from the tips of your toes, feeling so good in every way. And perhaps you notice, perhaps you notice the warmth. Perhaps certain areas of your body are beginning to feel warmer now. Perhaps you're directing some attention towards your right hand, and noticing how that hand feels, and as you do, it takes you down deeper, and it makes you consider and think about what it would be like to be outside, feeling the sun pour down on you, feeling comfortable, feeling secure in every way.

Maybe you begin to look up and you notice there's a feather falling, a feather flying gracefully in the air, down towards you, slowly, gracefully. As that feather drops, it drops you down deeper, so you can feel more confident, more secure, more relaxed, and it makes you imagine a time when you felt so good about yourself. Perhaps you could hear the sounds, the sounds of those times in your mind. You feel the warmth pouring over you from the sun, but you remember that with every word I say, it drops you down deeper so that you can feel better, and you notice that feather getting closer. The closer it gets to you, the further down you drop, feeling so good in every way.

I'm now going to begin counting down from five to one.

Each time I say a number, it will take you down twice as deep as the number before, twice as deep so that you can feel twice as good, twice as secure, twice as confident. And, with each number I say, it will take you down deeper, it will still your conscious mind, and every number I say will take you down to an area of security.

Five, deeper, relaxed, feeling so good in every way, just letting everything go. This is your time, a special time for you that you appreciate, that you're committed to for making change in your life. Four, deeper, relaxed, doubling that relaxation with each and every number, noticing how good you feel. Three, deeper now, profoundly relaxed, peaceful, feeling good in every way, appreciating the way you feel, appreciating that feather gracefully falling, dropping you down deeper with every movement it makes down.

Two, you, deeper relaxed. Now, this is a time for you, a time for you to make the changes you desire, and allowing you to experience a wonderful feeling of peace, profound serenity.

One, deeper, relax now, feeling so good in every way, and every easy breath you exhale, and every word I say takes you down deeper, so that you can feel better.

INSERT YOUR SPECIFIC SUGGESTIONS HERE (weight loss, stress, patience, smoking, etc.)

Soon, when I count from 1-5 you will return to being fully awake and aware. You will feel very good about yourself and the time we have spent together. By the time I reach the number 5 you will be fully awake and refreshed. You will be more aware and awake than when you started this session.

Your eyes will open easily only when you have accepted the belief of each suggestion you have been given.

1... more alert now wanting to move...

2... feeling refreshed...

3... becoming more aware of your surroundings...

4... noticing how good you feel...

5... wide awake and looking forward to your next session.

Wonderful!

7

The Future of Hypnosis

The future of hypnosis is bright. As science continues to discover more and more about the capacity of the brain, research is expanding to include the mind-body connection.

Hypnosis as a science and therapy can only benefit for this close analysis.

Recent Hypnotic Discoveries

Over the last several years there have been significant advances in neuroscience, which has allowed us to more effectively study hypnosis.

In fact, science has developed instruments for studying hypnosis. This has allowed hypnosis to come out of the dark ages and join the cognitive sciences from traditional medical and psychological organizations.

Many people are surprised to learn there is a measurement tool of hypnotic susceptibility. Before we go any further I'd like to share some information with you about the science behind hypnosis.

In the future, hypnosis will be more widely studied to learn more about the mind-body connection. Fascinating links between relaxation and meditation, and their positive impact on hypertension are currently being studied. Almost every medical science can at least look at hypnosis and the link between a person's will, their subconscious mind, and the bodily effects of the linking of the two.

In 1963, Basmajian discovered that hypnotized subjects could impact a single cell. There are also studies that show the relationship between brainwaves and the cells in our bodies. The results are undeniable.

Moving into the future, hypnosis will be extremely helpful in solving psychological problems. The use of hypnosis tools to better understand a person's attitudes, values, beliefs, and emotions through suggestion and imagery will be used to learn more about the mind-body connection.

There will also be a push in the future for more advanced education and training of hypnotherapists and hypnotists. The focus by medical governing bodies and the public will be for more advanced learning and study regarding the power of hypnosis and its impact on the human mind. A more comprehensive education for practitioners will probably be offered through advanced degree programs, and will have a comprehensive training curriculum that will include advanced biological study in addition to psychology.

8

The Misuse of Hypnosis

As soon as the practice of hypnosis was developed, there were people that began using it in ways that were not positive.

Hypnosis Ethics

There is sometimes an ethical fine line between the right and wrong uses of hypnosis in today's world. Advertisers plan their marketing campaigns to gain access to people's subconscious during times of the day where they are highly suggestible (early morning, late evening). By being aware of this and other underhanded misuse of hypnotic suggestion and trances, you can be aware of it and ensure that you maintain control of your own thoughts.

Improper Use of Hypnosis

You should not fear that you will lose control when you are hypnotized. As a matter of fact, fear is the greatest barrier to successfully being hypnotized. There is no evidence of a scientific nature that supports any claims that hypnosis makes a person take actions against their core fundamental values and morals. There is also no proof or evidence that hypnosis weakens a subject's willpower or makes a person dependent when they were not prior to hypnosis.

Hypnotized subjects will not use fantasies as a catalyst for behavior that conflicts with their ethical code. Hypnosis does not cause harm to subjects, and no cases have ever been medically documented to prove that it is harmful. It can be safely said, that through my experiences with decades of hypnosis experience, that it is in no way dangerous.

Many people fear hypnosis. Those fears are usually unwarranted. It is important to think carefully about any underlying fears that you might harbor about hypnosis. If you try to use hypnosis while having underlying fears, your experience will not work as you desire.

The top five myths about hypnosis are:

MYTH #1:

"Between the hypnotist and myself, I will be the less intelligent of us. Since I'll be in a vulnerable position, I'm concerned about being taken advantage of."

TRUTH:

Hypnosis is used to help people, and hypnotists go into the business to serve as a guide on the journey. When you are hypnotized you are not unconscious. You will never be asked to do or say anything that your subconscious mind doesn't want you to do. And regarding the levels of intelligence, by understanding the importance of working with your subconscious mind, you are actually more highly evolved and intelligent.

MYTH #2:

"I might get stuck in hypnosis and never be the same again."

TRUTH:

Hypnosis is not like it is in the movies. That's pure fiction. Hypnosis will only last as long as it is beneficial to you. This is just like any other state of consciousness – like sleeping, for example.

MYTH #3:

"Believing in the viability of hypnosis, and practicing it, means that I am gullible."

TRUTH:

Practicing hypnosis doesn't mean that you are easily swayed or foolish. Hypnosis helps you gain control of your life by working with your subconscious to give you more options and control in day-to-day interactions and activities.

MYTH #4:

"I'll lose control of myself and be made to quack like a duck."

TRUTH:

Control doesn't change hands during hypnosis. You will always have control over what you say and do. Hypnosis used as entertainment sometimes creates a show around participants doing funny things while they are under a hypnotic trance – hence the "quack like a duck" reference.

Understand that the only reason people participating in entertainment hypnosis and do the things that they do is because their core beliefs and attitudes agree with what the hypnotist is asking them to do.

No matter if you are practicing self-hypnosis or working with a hypnotist, you will always only select to follow the suggestions that feel right.

MYTH #5:

"When my subconscious mind is open and vulnerable, I will be susceptible to undesirable suggestions being placed in my subconscious mind."

TRUTH:

The way hypnosis works is to first open the subconscious mind, then use carefully worded suggestions to encourage a positive behavior. The catch is, you have to deep down want to make the change, or otherwise it won't work.

For example, smokers know they should/have to stop smoking but can't seem to get the willpower to do it. When you are hypnotized, the suggestions are focused on changing the beliefs and attitudes about stopping so that the behaviors can then follow. The fundamental belief in the subject is that all of the suggestions to stop smoking are right on. Your subconscious mind selects what is in alignment with your core values.

9

Conclusion

We are just now beginning to enter a phase where hypnosis will grow exponentially and improve the lives of those who utilize this powerful tool. I believe that with the current research that is possible in neuroscience, and the realization of both individuals and corporations that hypnosis can be extremely valuable, the horizon for hypnosis is brighter then ever.

I want to thank you for joining me and learning about hypnosis. I encourage you to begin to use this powerful tool to make the changes that will benefit you and create the life you desire. I'm certain that you will find your new life rewarding and exciting.

Consider visiting **www.hypnoticsciences.com**, where you will find a number of other hypnotic resources that I have authored.

I wish you much success personally and professionally and hope you will use the power of hypnosis to create a more rewarding future for yourself and your loved ones. I hope to see you soon in my audience. I look forward to hearing of your success!

Fun Facts About Hypnosis

Did you Know…

Over the last century and more, hypnosis has been fully explored and examined by many formal organizations such as:

• The Canadian Medical Association (CMA) formally recognized the therapeutic value of hypnosis in 1958.

• In 1892 the British Medical Association (BMA) formally recognized that hypnosis had applications in modern medicine.

• In 1958, the American Medical Association (AMA) declared hypnosis a useful medical tool.

• Sigmund Freud used hypnosis with his patients while developing his theories on psychoanalysis.

• In 1847, the Roman Catholic Church recognized hypnosis as a natural part of our own ability, and not the work of the devil. It stands by this claim today.

• People throughout the generations, worldwide, have recognized the value of the hypnotic trance.

A

Appendix A - Glossary

Abreaction - a reaction (considered involuntary) during hypnosis that causes the hypnotized person to release suppressed emotions usually related to a traumatic event in the person's past.

Age Regression – a condition created by the suggestion that the hypnotized person image a particular time or age in their past. Can also be used to regress to a past life. See Past Life Regression.

Alpha Waves – alpha waves are generated by the brain during the state of hypnosis, sometimes called the hypnoidal state. Alpha state is slower, or deeper, than the normal awake state (Beta State). It's also faster than the Theta state, which is considered a deeper hypnotic state. This occurs at 7-24 waves per second.

Analgesia – the hypnotic removal of the perception of pain.

Anchor – a distinct catalyst, such as a touch, image or even a word, that is associated with a particular thought, emotion or psychological state of mind.

Amnesia – creating the inability to remember specified events

Anaesthesia – hypnosis can simulate the complete removal of feeling in a specified area.

Auto Hypnosis – using hypnosis on oneself. Also see, Self Hypnosis.

Back of Room – products that you sale (usually after a show), traditionally in the back of the room, near the exit doors. Also called BOR.

Beta Waves – the brain waves generated during a normal waking state.

BOR – Back of Room. Also see, Back of Room.

Catalepsy - one of the hypnotic phenomenons, catalepsy is a state where the muscles of the body, in whole or in part, appear rigid. Usually hypnotists test for small muscle catalepsy first (eyes) and move on to larger muscle catalepsy (arms, etc.).

Clinical Hypnotherapy – the use of hypnosis for therapeutic reaons

Conscious (mind)- the reasoning part of the brain that is logical and responsible for decision making part of the mind. The conscious mind is what we use in an awake state.

Critical Factor – a part of the mind that acts as a guardian between the conscious and unconscious minds. It works to filter incoming information and deciding whether it should be passed from the conscious mind to the unconscious mind. Some theories propose that this passing of information from the conscious to unconscious takes place while we sleep.

Deepener – A technique used by a hypnotist to take the hypnotized person to a deeper level of hypnotic trance.

Delta – the waveform that happens during sleep, and the deepest levels of hypnosis. It is the slowest and deepest brain wave activity.

Direct Suggestion – Giving an overt suggestion given to a hypnotized person to do, think or experience something.

Double Bind – a technique where the hypnotized person is given two, so that their unconscious mind will generally choose the stronger of the suggestions, but where even the lesser of the suggestions is acceptable. Example: You may go into a medium trance, or you may go into a deep trance.

Emergence – the process of bringing someone from a deeper state of hypnosis to a lighter state of hypnosis, or completely out of hypnosis.

Ericksonian Hypnosis - A theory of hypnosis named after Milton Erickson.

Esdaile State – coined by Dave Elman, the Esdaile state is believed to be the deepest state of hypnosis currently known. It was named after James Esdaile.

Eye Accessing Cues - Studying the movements of the eyes which indicate visual, auditory or kinesthetic thinking when moving in certain directions.

Eye Fixation – a type of induction involving the person to be hypnotized staring at an object or place. The stereotypical swinging watch is an example of eye fixation.

Forensic Hypnosis - a applications of hypnosis typically used in the legal arena. Although testimony gotten while hypnosis generally cannot be used for testimony, law enforcement will sometimes use it to gather evidence by improving the recall of a witness.

Fractionation – the process of bringing a hypnotized person in and out of hypnosis in order to deepen the level of hypnosis. The Dave Elman induction uses fractionation to deepen the hypnosis by having the client open and close their eyes repeatedly.

Hypnoanalysis – a technique that uses hypnosis to discover psychological or emotional issues root cause.

Hypnoidal – the beginnings of trance state, or a very light state of trance.

Hypnosis – a technique whereby the hypnotized person goes into a state of increased concentration and relaxation, during which their critical factor is set aside allowing for increased suggestibility.

Hypnotherapist – a hypnotist who uses hypnosis for to help other overcome habits or issues.

Hypnotherapy – the practice of using hypnosis to help a client by facilitating positive change in their life by helping them overcome habits or issues.

Hypnotic Hangover – a condition of disorientation, sometimes caused by being emerged too quickly from hypnosis.

Hypnotic Trance – a state of relaxation and concentration marked by increased suggestibility

Hypnotism – See Also Hypnosis.

Ideo Motor Response (IMR) – an involuntary physical movement caused by the subconscious mind, commonly used to communicate with the unconscious.

 Indirect Suggestion – using a permissive or covert suggestion

Induction - the process of guiding a person into hypnotic trance.

Instant Induction – the fastest form of hypnotic induction

Law Of Compound Suggestions – A cascading method of reinforcing a suggestion by giving a weak suggestion, followed by another suggestion that reinforces it, followed by a third suggestion that reinforces the second, which further reinforces the first.

Mirroring – an NLP technique whereby one person simulates the body language of another in order to establish rapport.

Modelling – an NLP technique whereby a person studies and then imitates the behavior of another person, usually one who has already obtained the result that they are striving for.

Negative Hallucination – a suggestion to a hypnotized person that they will not perceive something that really exists

Neuro Pathways – a neural tract connecting one part of the brain to another part of the brain. The more we think about something, the stronger the neural pathway becomes.

Pacing – using the technique of mirroring to mimmick another's behavior, posture and/or speech patterns in order to build rapport.

Past-life Regression – the practice of age regressing a person to a time before their physical birth where they may see what took place to them in a previous lifetime. It is highly debatable whether what they see if real or a creation of the subconscious mind.

Patter – the Refers to the form of speech that the hypnotherapist will use whilst communicating with the subject during a hypnotic trance.

Positive Hallucination - When a hypnotised person sees what is not really there.

Post Hypnotic Suggestion - A suggestion made while a person is in hypnosis to be acted upon after the session. This may include stopping smoking, exercising more etc.

Pre-Induction – a reassuring talk done before the actual hypnosis. See also Pre-Talk.

Pre-Talk – a reassuring talk done before the actual hypnosis during a stage performance or street performance.

Progressive Relaxation - a hypnotic technique used to relax the entire body by focusing on specific areas of the body, and relaxing them one by one.

Rapid Induction – a very quick form of induction used to put a willing volunteer into trance.

Rapport – developing a relationship of mutual understand or trust between two people.

Script - A pre-written script of what a hypnotherapist will say during trance work. These are usually adapted to take into account the individuality of the client, and their particular goals.

Self Hypnosis – a technique whereby a person guides themselves into a hypnotic trance.

Shock Induction – a form of induction that uses a "shock," or suprises, to initiate hypnotic trance.

Somnambulism – a deep state of hypnotic trance.

Stage Hypnotist - a hypnotist who uses hypnosis to entertain others.

Speed Induction – a very quick form of induction. See also Rapid Induction.

Subconscious – the part of the mind that holds long term memory, core beliefs, etc. It is also responsible for involuntary body functions, such as making the heart beat and breathing. See also unconscious mind.

Time Distortion – a distortion of time in the mind of a hypnotized person to appear longer or shorter than the actual measurement of time.

Unconscious – another name for the subconscious mind. Many people use them interchangeably. See also Subconscious Mind.

Under – a vernacular express of being in the state of hypnosis.

Yes Set – a common technique where a person asks several questions where they know the answer will be an affirmative answer, in order to help convince the subject to agree to a suggestion by getting him in a affirmative mode of thinking.

B

Appendix B – Elman Induction

I've included a modified Dave Elman induction that you can also practice on others. It includes some testing so you can determine what level of hypnosis the person is experiencing.

Dave Elman was a stage hypnotist who taught hypnosis to hundreds of doctors around the country back in the early 1900's. His teachings are still followed today and the induction he created is still practical for today's hypnotherapy and has been used and modified by stage hypnotists alike.

I present a modified version of the Dave Elman Induction:

"In a moment, we're going to being the process that will allow you to go hypnosis. I don't know if you'll go into a light trance, a medium trance, or go into a deep trance.

The first step in going into hypnosis is to put your feet flat on the floor and put your hands on your legs so they are not touching.

Now, let's take a nice deep breath, filling your lungs all the way up, and hold it. And release it and allow your body to relax as you exhale.

Good. Now, take a deeper breath and hold it. And as you exhale, allow your body to relax even more.

Now, take the deepest breath of all, hold it. And as you release it, just allow your eyes to relax and close down.

Good.

Continue to relax your entire body with each easy breath you take.

I want you to concentrate on relaxing your eyelids. Relax those eyelids and all the muscles around your eyes. Relax them so completely that as long as you maintain that concentration, your eyes will remain shut. And when you have relaxed them to that point, I want you to test them and make sure that they will not open. Go and test those eyelids and find that they will not open. Really test those eyelids.

Good. Stop testing and take that sense of relaxation in your eyes and push it up to the top of your head and then let it roll down your body from the top of your head, all the way to the tips of your toes in a warm wave of relaxation. And notice how good it feels, just to let go and relax.

And as relaxed as you are at this moment, you can relax ten times deeper. In a moment, I'm going to ask you to open your eyes.

I'll then ask you to close them again. When they close, just allow yourself to drop down ten times deeper and become ten times more relaxed.

Open your eyes. And close them. Good. Ten times deeper.

Each time we do this, just allow that wonderful relaxing feeling to double and al-low yourself to go down ten times deeper.

Now, open your eyes. And close them down. Double that relaxation.

One more time. Open your eyes. And close them down, ten times deeper.

In a moment, I'm going to pick up your left arm. Allow that left arm to be loose, limp, and relaxed. Just like a wet dishrag. I know you could help me lift that arm, but don't. Let me do all the lifting.

(Lift arm)

Good. Really relax that arm. And in a moment, I'm going to drop this arm and when it touches your leg, just double that sense of relaxation you feel and allow yourself to go down even deeper.

(Drop arm)

Good. You're doing so well with the physical relaxation and now, we'll relax mentally.

When I ask you to, I want you to count backwards from 100. As you say each number, say deeper relaxed. With each number, allow your mind to become twice as relaxed, like the crystal clear waters of a smooth mountain lake. As your mind becomes more relaxed, you'll notice that the numbers just seem to disappear and by time you get to 96 or sooner, they'll be completely gone.

When I ask you to start counting backwards, I'd like you to count like this…

100… deeper relaxed…

99… deeper relaxed…

98…deeper relaxed…

And just let those numbers completely fade by time you get to 96, or sooner. And when they do, just notice how good that feels.

Begin counting…

Client: 100…deeper relaxed…

Client: 99…deeper relaxed…

Client: 98…deeper relaxed…

Client: 97…deeper relaxed…

Are they all gone?

Client: Yes.

Good, just allow yourself to sink down, even deeper.

And now, as I count backwards from 10 to 1, just allow your relaxation to double with each number I say.

10… Double that relaxation.

9…

8… Deeper relaxed

7..

6. That's right..

5.. Just allow that relaxation to double with every number I say and every easy breath you take.

4..

3.. Good.

2..

1.. Allow yourself to relax completely… and go much deeper. Good.

(Testing – Small muscle catalepsy)

And now, I want you to focus in on the muscles of your eyes. Relax those eyelids to a point where they will not open. Relax them so completely, that they become stuck shut. In fact, if you were to try to open them, the harder you try to open them, the more stuck they become. Try to open them and find that you can't.

(Watch for movement of the eyebrows and eyelids to make sure they're testing).

Now relax those eyelids and go much deeper. That's right.

(Testing – Large muscle catalepsy)

In a moment, I'm going to lift up your right arm (you can use either arm).

(Lift up arm)

I want you to make this arm stiff and rigid, as if it were made out of a piece of steel. Stiff and rigid as if it were made out of steel. (Touch shoulder) Your shoulder is locked tight, stiff and rigid. (Touch elbow) Your elbow is locked tight, stiff and rigid. (Touch wrist) Your wrist is locked tight, stiff and rigid.

You arm if stiff and rigid. In fact, it's so stiff and rigid, that if you were to TRY to bend it, the more you TRY to bend it, the more STIFF and RIGID it becomes. The more STIFF and RIGID it becomes. Try to bend it and find that you can't. TRY to bend it and find that you CAN'T.

Good, stop trying. When I touch your arm, it will go completely loose, limp and relaxed and you'll go much deeper.

(Lightly push down on their arm and it should go loose and fall to their lap)

I'm going to take your hand and put it on your leg. When I do that, your hand will become stuck to your leg. Stuck to your leg as if with super glue. When I put your hand on your leg, that hand will become stuck, as if superglued to your leg.

(Pick up hand and put it on their leg)

You hand is glued, STUCK to your leg. It's like your hand and your leg are carved from the same piece of marble. In fact, if you were to TRY to move that hand, the more you try, the more STUCK it becomes. The more STUCK it becomes. STUCK and GLUED. Try to move that hand and find that you can't. Try to move that hand and find that you can't.

Good. Stop trying.

(Test for depth)

In moment, I'm going to have to open your eyes. You'll stay completely in trance, but I when I could to three, I want you to open your eyes and look down at your stuck hand. I'll then ask you to try to move the stuck hand but you will find that no matter how hard you try, your hand remains stuck... STUCK, as if superglued. The more you try, the more stuck it becomes.

1... 2... 3... Open your eyes and look at your hand. Try to move that hand and find that you can't. TRY to move that hand and find that you can't.

Good, stop trying. Close down your eyes and go much deeper. When I touch your hand, it becomes unstuck and goes loose limp and relaxed.

(Touch hand)

In a moment, I'm going to snap my fingers. When I do, it's going to be as if the number four never existed. The number four never existed. The number 3 is so close to the number 5 that another number couldn't possibly be between them. When I snap my fingers, the number four is gone. When you count, you will count 1..2.. 3.. 5... 6.

When I snap my fingers, the number four is gone.

(*snap singers*)

I want you to count aloud from 1 to 10. Start counting now.

(Listen to their counting. They should skip the number 4)

Good. In a moment, I'm going to count from 1 to 3. When I say the number 3, I want you to open your eyes and stay fully in trance.

1..2..3.

(Wait for them to open up their eyes)

I want you to count your fingers for me aloud.

(Point to each of their fingers and have them count each one as you point to it. Again, they should skip 4. Sometimes they will just skip 4 and sometimes they will count 6 fingers on their hand.)

Good. Now, close your eyes and go much deeper. That's right.

When I snap my fingers again, the number 4 will be back. It will be back be-tween 3 and 5. When I snap my fingers, the number 4 is back.

(*snap singers*)

I want you to count from 1 to 5 for me aloud.

(Wait for them to count to make sure 4 is back for them)

Good!

(Emerge them)

In a moment, I will begin counting up from 1 to 5. As I say each number, you will become more aware and awake. When I say the number 5, you will be wide awake, fully alert and be filled with energy, as if you've just had a 2 hour nap.

1… You begin to become more of your surroundings.

2…

3… Starting to feel more energic and more alert.

4…

5…. Wide awake, feeling great!

Of course, instead of doing the testing, you can substitute your suggestions immediately after the deepening, or you may do the testing to see what level of trance they are at and to prove to the person that they were hypnotized.

The important thing is that you practice and learn how to read the signs of trance and how to adjust the induction to suit the person you are trying to hypnotize.

For more information on Dave Elman and the Dave Elman induction, I high recommend Sean Michael Andrews DVD series on the Dave Elman induction as well as his DVD series on Dave Elman.

Both are available for purchase on Sean's website at: www.worldsfastesthypnotist.com

Work Cited

Works Cited and Research on Hypnosis

The Stanford Hypnotic Susceptibility Scales
http://ist-socrates.berkeley.edu/~kihlstrm/hypnosis_research.htm

Proc Natl Acad Sci U S A. 1998 Feb 17;95(4):1956-60.

Where the imaginal appears real: a positron emission tomography study of auditory hallucinations.

Szechtman H, Woody E, Bowers KS, Nahmias C.

Psychosom Med. 1969 May-Jun;31(3):227-46.

The nature of hypnotic analgesia and placebo response to experimental pain. McGlashan TH, Evans FJ, Orne MT.

Int J Clin Exp Hypn. 2001 Apr;49(2):83-94.

Page 138 The Hypnosis Handbook

Is the hypnotized subject complying. Kinnunen T, Zamansky HS, Nordstrom BL.

Int J Clin Exp Hypn. 2008 Apr;56(2):119-42.

Measuring hypnotizability: the case for self-report depth

scales and normative data for the long Stanford scale.
Wagstaff GF, Cole JC, Brunas-Wagstaff J.

Int J Clin Exp Hypn. 2000 Apr;48(2):138-53.
A meta-analysis of hypnotically induced analgesia: how
effective is hypnosis? Montgomery GH, DuHamel KN,
Redd WH.

Int J Clin Exp Hypn. 1996 Jan;44(1):33-51.Links
Hypnosis treatment of clinical pain: understanding why
hypnosis is useful. Holroyd J.

Int J Clin Exp Hypn. 1997 Jul;45(3):251-65.
The state of the "state" debate in hypnosis: a view from the
cognitive-behavioral perspective. Chaves JF.

Am J Clin Hypn. 2000 Jan-Apr;42(3-4):274-92.
The response set theory of hypnosis. Kirsch I.

Am J Clin Hypn. 1997 Jul;40(1):329-48.
Hypnotic involuntariness and the automaticity of everyday
life. Kirsch I, Lynn SJ.

Int J Clin Exp Hypn. 1995 Oct;43(4):386-98.

Making hypnosis happen: the involuntariness of the hypnotic experience. Zamansky HS, Ruehle BL.

Int J Clin Exp Hypn. 1993 Jul;41(3):225-33.
The phenomenology of the experiences and the depth of hypnosis: comparison of direct and indirect induction techniques. Szabó C.

Conscious Cogn. 2005 Jun;14(2):304-15.
Does 'hypnosis' by any other name smell as sweet? The efficacy of 'hypnotic' inductions depends on the label 'hypnosis'. Gandhi B, Oakley DA.

Am J Clin Hypn. 2002 Jan-Apr;44(3-4):231-40.
Defining hypnosis as a trance vs. cooperation: hypnotic inductions, suggestibility, and performance standards. Lynn SJ, Vanderhoff H, Shindler K, Stafford J.

Conscious Cogn. 2008 Mar;17(1):240-53. Epub 2007 Jun 18. Is hypnotic suggestibility a stable trait? Fassler O, Lynn SJ, Knox J.

Conscious Cogn. 2003 Jun;12(2):219-30.
Seeing is believing: the reality of hypnotic hallucinations.

Bryant RA, Mallard D.

Int J Clin Exp Hypn. 1989 Jan;37(1):15-30.

Changes in body attitude as a function of posthypnotic suggestions. Van Denburg EJ, Kurtz RM.

Int J Psychophysiol. 1993 Sep;15(2):153-66.

EEG spectral analysis during hypnotic induction, hypnotic dream and age regression. De Pascalis V.

Smoke Free Forever

You too can learn – How to Stop Smoking Permanently!

Finally, a program for those who want to quit smoking and for smokers who have tried to quit and failed! If you have the desire to stop smoking, John Cressman's program provides a powerful step by step formula to become a non-smoker.

Eliminate cravings for cigarettes and increase the quality of your life while you reprogram yourself to be 100% free of all tobacco urges, permanently.

Listen and watch your life change for the better! The Trance State Hypnosis Program helps you to:

• Quit smoking effortlessly

• Be free of all smoking desires

• Feel good about yourself

• Enjoy a healthier lifestyle

• Acquire more time

• Save more than $2500 per year (one pack a day habit)

• Become healthier, happier and more active

If you have tried to quit smoking, thought about giving up cigarettes or are unable to enroll in John Cressman's live programs, you can "Stop Smoking Now" simply by listening to this recording.

Check out: www.hypnoticsciences.com for more information.

Perfect Weight

MAINTAIN YOUR IDEAL WEIGHT, FOREVER

Take control of your weight. Even if past diets and efforts have failed, now you can lose the weight you want and keep it off.

John Cressman helps people conquer their bad habits and empowers them to overcome obstacles to permanent weight loss. His stimulating, self help program using exclusive "sensory enhanced" trance state hypnosis technology help you become thinner and experience better health by dramatically changing your eating habits.

The LOSE WEIGHT AND FEEL GREAT program empowers you to:

- Lose the weight you want

- Look fit and trim

- Feel better about yourself

- Increase energy levels

- Stay motivated indefinitely

- Decrease health risks

Listen to this program beginning today and make the weight changes you desire, immediately!

Check out: www.hypnoticsciences.com for more information.

Stress Free

You too can learn – the stress management system!

The National Institute for Occupational Safety and Health (NIOSH) has recently acknowledged that the nature of work is changing at whirlwind speed. Perhaps now more than ever, job stress poses a serious threat to workers and, in turn, to the health of organizations.

In addition, stress has been known to cause family discord, financial troubles, professional difficulties and relationship issues.

John Cressman's Stress Management Program allows you to immediately dissolve the stress you feel and provides a tool to handle future stress, in a healthy manner!

The Stress Management Program benefits include:

- Tremendous calming effects

- Deep relaxation techniques

- Powerful ways to increase productivity

- Enjoy a healthier lifestyle

- Stronger and meaningful relationships

- Increased personal satisfaction

- Overall life balance

Check out: www.hypnoticsciences.com for more information.

Become a Stage Hypnotist

Now… you too can become a stage hypnotist!

Let certified stage hypnotist John Cressman show you how to go from knowing nothing about hypnosis to performing your first hypnosis show in 30 days.

Zero to Stage Hypnotist in 30 Days is a revolutionary new book that includes everything you need to get started in this exciting career!

You'll learn:

- How to hypnotize others

- Hypnotizing groups

- Where to perform

- How to get your first booking

- How to get publicity

Look for *Zero to Stage Hypnosis in 30 Days* in your favorite bookstore, on Amazon.com or check out: **www.zerotostagehypnotist.com** for more information.

Get Hypnosis on the Go

Want to use hypnosis to make changes in the your life? Do you have any iPhone?

Now, you can get hypnosis on the go with **Pocket Hypnosis** for the iPhone and iPod Touch through the Apple iTunes Store.

Choose From:

> • **Pocket Hypnosis Dating Pak for Him/Her** – get rid of fear and anxiety when meeting members of the opposite sex
>
> • **Pocket Hypnosis Student Pak** – use the power of hypnosis to improve your academic performance
>
> • **Pocket Hypnosis Abundance Pak** – use the law of attraction and the power of hypnosis to achieve your goals
>
> • **Pocket Hypnosis Financial Pak** – use the law of attraction and the power of hypnosis to attract money into your life
>
> • **Pocket Hypnosis Max** – A custom hypnotic experience that lets you choose your suggestions, music, induction and more!

To find out more, search for **Pocket Hypnosis** or John Raven in the Apple iTunes Store! Try it for free with **Pocket Hypnosis Lite**!

Other Hypnotic Resources

Hypnotic Sciences

www.hypnoticsciences.com

WestWard Publishing website

www.westwardpublishing.com

Stage Hypnosis Center

www.stagehypnosiscenter.com

Subliminal Sciences

www.subliminalscience.com

World's Fastest Hypnotist

www.worldsfastesthypnotist.com

Keys to the Mind

www.keystothemind.com

National Guild of Hypnotists

www.ngh.net

Harvard University Gazette

http://www.news.harvard.edu/gazette/2000/08.21/hypnosis.html

Stanford Online Report

http://www.stanford.edu/dept/news/report/news/september6/hypnosis-96.html

Scientific American

http://www.sciam.com/2001/0701issue/0701nash.html

Study of Healthcare Organizations and Transactions

http://www.institute-shot.com/hypnosis_and_health.htm

Study of Healthcare Organizations and Transactions

http://www.sunsite.utk.edu/IJCEH

About the Author

Hypnotist John Cressman is one of America's top hypnotic entertainers, performing regularly from coast to coast. The busy schedule keeps him in demand for groups of all types – high schools, corporate functions, festivals and other functions.

Besides delighting audiences across the country, John Cressman also teaches hypnosis for self-improvement, weight loss, stress management and more at both Lehigh Carbon Community College and Northampton Community College.

Cressman is a graduate of the American School of Hypnosis and is a certified instructor for the Northeast American School of Hypnosis. He is also certified as a hypnotherapist with the America International Association of Hypnosis, as well as the International Hypnosis Association. In addition, he has received advanced instruction in stage hypnosis and is certified as a stage hypnotist by the Stage Hypnosis Center.

He is the author of numerous self-hypnosis audio programs that people can follow at home to achieve their goals. John is also the creator of the hypnotic iPhone application series Pocket Hypnosis under the name *John Raven* and has used them to help thousands of people worldwide.

To see if John Cressman is available for your next event or to schedule a hypnosis seminar for your company call 800-845-6097.

www.ingramcontent.com/pod-product-compliance
Lightning Source LLC
Chambersburg PA
CBHW021337090426
42742CB00008B/635